THE CASE AGAINST THE IRAN DEAL

How Can We Now Stop Iran from Getting Nukes?

by Alan Dershowitz

Rosetta Press
NEW YORK: 2015

A GATESTONE PUBLICATION
INSTITUTE

THE CASE AGAINST THE IRAN DEAL:

HOW CAN WE NOW STOP IRAN FROM GETTING NUKES?

Copyright © 2015 by Alan Dershowitz

Many chapters in this book were originally written and published as op-eds in various publications. Where this is the case, the date of original publication is given as an endnote to the chapter title.

∞ This paper meets the requirements of ANSI/NISO Z39.48-1992 (Permanence of Paper).

First edition published 2015 by RosettaBooks.

Cover design by Jay McNair. Cover photo by Shutterstock / Rob d, edited by Peter Clark.

Interior design by Brehanna Ramirez.

ISBN-13: 978-0-7953-4756-6

Library of Congress Control Number: 2015948024

www.RosettaBooks.com

This book is lovingly dedicated to my wife,
Carolyn Cohen, who helped me in so many ways
to write, edit, and produce it.

TABLE OF CONTENTS

ACKNOWLEDGMENTS

This book could not have been produced so quickly without the enormous help of Nicholas Maisel, who helped me with the research, my wife, Carolyn Cohen, who provided invaluable assistance in organizing the manuscript, and Maura Kelly, who did most of the typing. My loyal assistant over many years, Sarah Neely, also assisted. My constant acknowledgment to my children for their encouragement and constructive criticism. My appreciation as well to Danny Grossman, who arranged my contacts with Israeli officials, and to Alan Rothfeld for his meticulous input. And finally, to all those who are contributing to the important debate on this critical issue.

THE CASE AGAINST THE IRAN DEAL

The greatest danger the world faces in the twenty-first century is an Iranian nuclear arsenal. Accordingly, the critical question about the agreement recently negotiated with Iran is whether it makes it more likely or less likely that Iran will develop nuclear weapons in the foreseeable future. That is why this nuclear deal may be the most important—and dangerous—policy decision of the twenty-first century, and why all people who seek peace and security must focus on the agreement and what it portends for the future of the world. That is the subject of this book.

There can be little doubt about the dangers that would be posed by a nuclear armed Iran that already has the capacity to fire missiles into Israel, which it has threatened to annihilate, and into Sunni Arab countries that it seeks to dominate. Its leaders must be taken at their words when they express their hostile aggressiveness and determination to rule a Middle East free of Israel.

In 2004, it was reported that the former president of Iran, Hashemi Rafsanjani, a supposed moderate, had "boast[ed] [to an American journalist that] if Iran were to develop nuclear weapons and use them to attack Israel, they "would kill as many as five million Jews." He estimated that even if Israel retaliated by dropping its own nuclear bombs, Iran would probably lose only fifteen million people, which he said "would be a small 'sacrifice' from among the billion Muslims in the world."[1] The journalist said that Rafsanjani seemed pleased with his formulations. He later elaborated on his boast by stating "the dropping of one atomic bomb would not leave anything in Israel," but that an Israeli nuclear retaliation would just produce "damages in the Muslim world." This "moderate" former president of Iran continued: "it is not irrational to contemplate such an eventuality."[2]

In other words, the "not irrational" calculation being contemplated by at least some Iranian leaders is that since Israel is a "one bomb country," most of whose population (presumably including its 20 percent Arab population) would be killed by one bomb, and since Iran is a far larger country and part of the enormous "Muslim world," the trade-off might be worth it, especially to an apocalyptic regime that was prepared to sacrifice hundreds of thousands of its citizens—including thousands of child "soldiers"—in a futile war with Iraq. Would not such a regime equally be willing to sacrifice millions of its citizens to achieve its major political and religious imperative: namely the annihilation of the nation-state of the Jewish people?

Nor is Israel Iran's only potential nuclear target. Several prominent voices within the US and Israeli intelligence communities have warned that Iran is working to develop ICBMs capable of reaching the US. Iran has already tested medium-range ballistic missiles capable of reaching anywhere in the Middle East and much of Europe.[3] If their missiles are nuclearized—as they could be within ten years or sooner—there is no end to the damage Iran can threaten and deliver. That is why the potential of an Iran armed with a nuclear arsenal poses the greatest threat we have confronted in this century—a threat comparable to that posed by a rearmed Germany in the 1930s.

President Obama, himself, seemed to agree—before his election to a second term—that were Iran ever to develop nuclear weapons, it would be a "game changer," and he promised that he would "do whatever it takes" and "everything that's required" to "eliminate" this "grave" and "real" "security threat not only to the region but to the US."[4]

I have been writing and lecturing about the threat posed by Iran's quest for a nuclear arsenal for more than a decade. I have discussed it with President Obama, with his national security staff, with Prime Minister Netanyahu, with high-ranking members of Israel's military and intelligence communities, and with leading diplomats, scholars, journalists, and others. I have heard all sides of the issue presented intelligently, passionately, morally, and strategically. Now it is time for me to present the results of this decade-long encounter with the Iranian nuclear weapons program.

Let me begin with the nature of the deal itself. It is, in effect, a peace treaty between Iran and the P5 plus one (the US, Great Britain, France, Russia, and China, which are permanent members of the Security Council, plus Germany). As an alternative to the continuation of sanctions or the possibility of military action, the Iranians have agreed to certain limitations on the nuclear program they claim is for peaceful purposes—a claim almost no one believes. Although it is treaty-like in its language and effect, and although it may be considered a treaty under international law,* the Obama administration insists it is not a

---

* There is some debate as to the status of the agreement under international law given the Obama administration's refusal to acknowledge it as an official treaty. Nonetheless, various factors, namely the intention of the negotiating parties, and the endorsement of the agreement by the Security Council, render it analogous to a treaty for the purposes

treaty under US domestic law, because if it were, it would require ratification by two-thirds of the Senate—an unlikely prospect. But if it is not a treaty, then it would require a two-thirds vote of both houses to override the veto President Obama has promised to employ if Congress were to enact legislation disapproving of the deal. In other words, the outcome depends on whether it is a "treaty," as that word is used in our Constitution. If it is, it will almost certainly not be ratified. If it is not, it will probably not be rejected by legislation that is subject to a Presidential veto.

The Constitution does not define the word "treaty," presumably leaving its definition to history, precedent, and practice. There is little legal precedent on this precise issue because courts are reluctant to intrude on disputes between the executive and legislative branches. But history and practice give the president leeway in deciding what to call an international agreement. If the president denominates it a "treaty," then it must be ratified by two-thirds of the Senate, and it becomes the law of the land, binding on future administrations unless it is rescinded or expires by its own terms. If the president calls it an "executive agreement," he need not submit it to the Senate as a matter of constitutional obligation. But pursuant to the Iran Nuclear Agreement Review Act of 2015—called the Corker Bill—Congress will, in

---

of international law. For an in-depth discussion, see Andrew McCarthy, "Congress Must Ditch the Corker Bill and Treat the Iran Deal as Either a Treaty or Proposed Legislation to be Voted Up or Down," *The National Review*, 17 July 2015; Andrew McCarthy, "Responding to Jack Goldsmith on the Corker Bill & the Nature of Obama's Iran Deal," *The National Review*, 20 April 2015; Jack Goldsmith, "The Complicated Politics of the Iran Review Act (And Why I Think They Cut in Favor of the Act)," Lawfare Blog, 14 July 2015; Amber Phillips, "Can Congress Stop the Iran Deal?", *Washington Post Online*, 14 July 2015.

the words of Speaker John Boehner, have a "role in reviewing any potential agreement regarding Iran's nuclear weapons program." The bill was approved in the Senate by a vote of 98 to 1, with only Senator Tom Cotton of Arkansas voting against the Corker Bill, arguing that "a nuclear-arms agreement with any adversary—especially the terror-sponsoring Islamist Iranian regime—should be submitted as a treaty and obtain a two-thirds majority vote in the Senate as required by the Constitution." The House of Representatives voted 400 to 25 for the law and the president signed it.

Under the law, a simple majority can vote to disapprove the deal, but the president can veto such a disapproval vote, and his veto could be overridden only by a two-thirds vote of both houses.

The stakes are so high, and the deal so central to the continuing security of the free world, that it should—as a matter of democratic governance—require more than a presidential agreement and one-third plus one of one house of Congress. But the way our Constitution is written, it is either a treaty or a presidential agreement. Under our Constitution, there is no intermediate position under which a simple majority rules.

In practice a hybrid third way has developed over time: the legislative-executive agreement, under which the president acts with a simple majority approval of both houses. Historically, it has been the prerogative of the president whether to act alone, under a "sole executive agreement," or with the approval of Congress, under a "legislative-executive agreement." Democratic principles of governance would suggest that the better practice in a situation like the Iran deal—which is of considerable duration and great strategic importance—would have been for President Obama to seek a legislative-executive agreement, but he has chosen not to, and by enacting the Corker Bill, Congress seems to have approved this decision. By requiring a two-thirds majority vote to reject this treaty-like agreement, the president has turned the constitution on its head.

Let us never forget, however, that America is a democracy, where the people rule, and if the majority of Americans oppose the deal, it will ultimately be rejected, if not by this administration, then by the next. In the end, the court of public opinion decides important policy decisions that may affect us all.*

And it is difficult to imagine a decision with higher stakes than whether to accept or reject this deal. If the deal succeeds, it may prevent the nation that leads the world in exporting terrorism from constructing a nuclear umbrella under which its terrorist surrogates can more freely terrorize the world. It may also prevent a nuclear confrontation between Israel, the only nation Iran has explicitly sworn to annihilate, and the fundamentalist tyranny that threatens its very existence. Finally, it may strengthen the hands of Iranian "moderates" and help create some degree of rapprochement between the Islamic Republic and the international community.[6]

Those are the important potential upsides to the deal. And they may come about if the deal actually stops Iran from *ever*—or over a very long period of time—developing the nuclear arsenal it is currently planning to develop and possibly deploy. The

---

* For example, the nuclear agreement with North Korea (the Agreed Framework between the United States of America and the Democratic People's Republic of Korea) negotiated by the Clinton administration was not implemented by Congress, many of whose members were opposed to the deal. See Glenn Kessler, "Cotton's Misguided History Lesson on the North Korean Nuclear Deal," *Washington Post Online,* 13 March 2015.

text of the deal itself begins with a very positive statement: an article of the "Preamble and General Provisions" unequivocally declares, "under no circumstances will Iran ever seek, develop, or acquire any nuclear weapons…."[,7] Yet defenders of the deal rarely quote or rely on that provision, suggesting that this language may be viewed as merely hortatory rather than as an integral or enforceable component to the agreement. There is nothing in the agreement itself that suggests the "Preamble and General Provisions" are non-binding. However, while preambles are important in that they assert the intention of the negotiating parties,[†] they are generally understood to be non-operative components to international treaties, and therefore to have "lesser binding value." Whether or not these words are binding as a technical matter of law,[‡] they represent a public reaffirmation by the Iranian government of its intentions in entering into this agreement. If Iran does not in fact have those intentions, the public ought to be aware of that. The public must also now be told whether the other signatories to the agreement understand

---

[*]   These words also appear in the preface of the deal, thereby emphasizing their importance.

[†]   Generally, the purpose of a preamble is to describe the objective and intent of a particular Convention; Article 31 of the Vienna Convention on the Law of Treaties states that "1. A treaty shall be interpreted in good faith in accordance with the ordinary meaning to be given to the terms of the treaty in their context and in light of its object and purpose. 2. The context for the purpose of the interpretation of a treaty shall comprise, in addition to the text… its preamble and annexes…."

[‡]   The heading "Preamble and General Provisions" itself is confusing: whereas preambles are generally considered non-binding, general provisions can sometimes be viewed as operative elements in treaties. Whether this was deliberately intended to be ambiguous is unclear; Congress should seek clarification.

that Iran has agreed never to seek nuclear weapons—even after the various time frames of the deal expire.

The downside of the deal is the likelihood that in exchange for a relatively brief moratorium on its nuclear weapons program, the deal will enhance Iran's economic capacity to export terrorism and threaten its neighbors—President Obama has acknowledged as much on several occasions.[8] Even more important, it may increase the chances that Iran will develop nuclear weapons lawfully within a relatively short time frame.

It is unrealistic to believe that any deal could prevent Iran from *ever* developing nuclear weapons. "Ever" is a long time, and few deals endure forever. So the success or failure of any deal will always be a matter of degree. We can say with absolute assurance that President Clinton's 1994 deal with North Korea was an abject failure, since that rogue nation immediately began to cheat and within a few short years had developed and tested a nuclear weapon. We can also conclude, with relative confidence, that the various strategic arms limitations agreements between the US and the former Soviet Union were a success, since they have remained in place for many years, despite some apparent mutual cheating around the edges. No deal is perfect, but some are worse than others, as evidenced by the North Korea fiasco. A key question, therefore, is whether this deal is closer to the one with North Korea or with the Soviet Union. There are no perfect analogies, but comparisons may still be quite informative.

To begin with, the current deal with Iran is unclear with regard to its intended duration. President Obama, in his statement announcing the agreement, described it as a "long-term deal with Iran that will prevent it from obtaining a nuclear weapon,"[9] thus implying that under this deal Iran will never—or at least not for a very long time—be allowed to become a nuclear weapons power. But critics of the deal point to language in the deal itself that suggests a much shorter time frame—anywhere from 8½ to 10 to 15 years.* President Obama himself, in an earlier interview, raised the "fear" that in "year 13, 14, 15, they have advanced centrifuges that enrich uranium fairly rapidly, and at that point the breakout times would have shrunk almost down to zero."[10] The State Department was forced to issue an unconvincing "clarification" of the president's ambiguous word, claiming that the president "was referring to a scenario in which there is no deal."[11] But that clarification is highly questionable, since the president has repeatedly said that without a deal, Iran could quickly—within months—be able to develop nuclear weapons, and his discussion of the "year 13, 14, 15" is clearly a reference to the time frame of the deal. As a lead article in the *New York Times*—which strongly supports the deal—put it: "Mr. Obama had already given ammunition to critics of a deal when he said in an April 2015 interview that after 13 years of the accord, Iran's breakout time could be down to nearly zero. That seemed to acknowledge the main critique of the emerging agreement— that it constituted the medium-term *management* of the Iranian program, not its *elimination*."[12]

---

* For example, an op-ed published in the *New York Times* by a respected nuclear proliferation expert, before the agreement was announced, estimated that under the expected terms of the deal, Iran's breakout time would in fact be no longer than 3 months; see Alan J. Kuperman, "The Iran Deal's Fatal Flaw," *New York Times*, 23 June 2015; an earlier article, co-written by the former Deputy Director for Safeguards of the IAEA estimated the breakout time to be "seven or eight months rather than a full year." Olli Heinonen and Simon Henderson, "There's a Huge Problem with Obama's Claims about Iranian Nuclear Breakout under a Final Deal," *Business Insider*, 17 June 2015.

Moreover, just hours after he assured the world that under the deal "Iran will not be able to develop a nuclear weapon," President Obama told Thomas L. Friedman that he should be judged "on one thing": "Does this deal prevent Iran from breaking out with a nuclear weapon *for the next 10 years*, and is that a better outcome for America, Israel, and our Arab allies than any other alternative on the table?"[13]). Why did the president talk about "the next ten years" if the deal itself explicitly prohibits Iran from "ever" pursuing nuclear weapons? What are we not being told?

The reality is that we do not know whether the deal provides for a relatively brief moratorium—a "middle-term management"—on Iran's development of nuclear weapons on the order of 8½ to 10 or 15 years, or whether it contemplates a longer-term *stoppage* of its nuclear weapons program, on the order of a quarter century or more. In his statement announcing the deal, President Obama conveyed the impression that this is a very long-term stoppage, while the Iranians and the deal's critics are insisting that this is merely a brief delay followed by a green light for Iran to do whatever it wishes. Absolute transparency on this question is as essential as it is lacking.

President Obama's second challenge—to judge him on whether this deal is "a better outcome... than any other alternative on the table,"[14]—begs the important question of whether we could have secured an even better (or less worse) outcome if we had not taken other options so quickly off the table during the negotiations. Following President Obama's reelection in 2012, we began to send the message to the Iranians that our military option was, for all practical purposes, off the table. We repeatedly announced that there are no military actions capable of stopping Iran's nuclear program.[15] For example, in an interview on Israeli television, President Obama said: "I can, I think, demonstrate, not based on any hope but on facts and evidence and analysis, that the best way to prevent Iran from having a nuclear weapon is a verifiable, tough agreement. A military solution will not fix it. Even if the United States participates, it would temporarily slow down an Iranian nuclear program but it will not eliminate it....."[16] We also told them that if no deal was struck, the tough sanctions regime then in place would begin to weaken and fall apart. Having eliminated the most important "sticks," we were left with the "carrot" of ending the sanctions altogether and eliminating the arms embargo enacted by the Security Council. This placed us in a weak bargaining position, the result of which is a weak deal.

So, no! President Obama should *not* be judged on whether *this* deal is less bad than the alternatives *currently* "on the table." He should be judged on whether this is the best deal his administration could have achieved. We may now be in the unenviable position of having to choose between a bad deal that will allow Iran to develop a nuclear arsenal in 10 years (or 8½ or 13) or an even worse outcome that will allow Iran to begin that process even sooner. If we were to judge President Obama "on one thing," that thing would be how he got us into a situation where we may be forced to accept a bad deal because the alternative may be worse.

A front page article in the *New York Times* of 16 July 2015, makes it clear that by taking the military option off the table, the US was bargaining with Iran as *an equal party*, rather than as a relatively weak adversary anxious to end all crippling sanctions and "keep their honor" while maintaining its status as a threshold nuclear power.[17] We surrendered our major advantage by publicly acknowledging our unwillingness to attack Iran if they do not accept the deal.

Yes, President Obama stated that no options, including the military, were off the table, but as the negotiations went on, nobody believed him, especially the Iranians. His claim that he doesn't bluff was itself seen as a transparent bluff. We negotiated not from military strength—our most significant advantage— but from an admission, and a false one at that, of military weakness, by publicly declaring that we were militarily incapable of permanently ending Iran's nuclear weapons program.

That "admission" is demonstrably false, as a matter of *military capability*, though it is an accurate description of the *Obama policy*. It may well be true that a single air attack would set back the Iranian program by only a few years, as President Obama has publicly claimed.[18] But we could have announced that the military option would include repeated air attacks on any nuclear weapons facility that Iran would build over the years. The point would have been that we will *never* allow Iran to develop nuclear weapons as long as they remain an outlaw theocratic tyranny that exports terrorism, supports Syria, employs terrorist surrogates in Lebanon, Yemen, and Gaza, and threatens to annihilate Israel. If the Iranian regime believed that there was a credible threat of military action that would prevent them from developing nuclear weapons, then they would have understood that it was foolish and self-destructive to continue to suffer from crippling sanctions. Economic pain alone would never have compelled Iran to give up its nuclear ambitions, but sanctions combined with the realization that we would *never* allow them to develop nuclear weapons, even if it took a military strike to stop them, would more likely have achieved that goal.

Instead we told the Iranian leaders that because *one* military strike could not permanently stop their nuclear weapons program, they do not have to worry about *any* military action by the US. That important concession invited them to negotiate with us *as equals*. What a terrible negotiating strategy for a superpower! Several days after I made this point in an op-ed in the *Boston Globe,* Thomas L. Friedman of the *New York Times* essentially repeated it in his op-ed, though he attributed the initial decision to remove the military option to President George W. Bush: "From the minute Iran detected that the US was unwilling to use its overwhelming military force to curtail Tehran's nuclear program—and that dates back to the George W. Bush administration… no perfect deal overwhelmingly favorable to America and its allies was ever going to emerge…."[19] He also adopted an argument I had made in September 2013 in an article in *Haaretz*[20]: "Congress should pass a resolution authorizing this and future presidents to use force to prevent Iran from ever becoming a nuclear weapons state." Such a resolution, in Friedman's opinion, would back up the "wager" the President has placed by agreeing to this imperfect deal.

Whether or not President Bush removed the military option when he was president—and I believe he did not but his Secretary of Defense Robert Gates did—there can be little doubt that President Obama spoke very differently about the possible use of force to prevent Iran from developing nuclear weapons *before* and *after* his reelection, and especially following the midterm election of 2014, which placed both houses under Republican control. Before his reelection, he repeatedly promised "to do whatever it takes" to prevent Iran from crossing the nuclear threshold, including the use of military force.[21] Jeffrey

Goldberg, who has interviewed President Obama several times about Iran, reported that he, Goldberg,

> "run[s] into people constantly who believe the bluffer in this relationship is Obama. Their argument holds that Obama will move toward a strategy of containment soon after the election, and there is no way he would ever use military force to prevent Iran from getting the bomb."[22]

Goldberg used Obama's own words to rebut that argument and to explain why he is "in the camp of people, however, who take him at his word, in part because he's repeated himself on the subject so many times and in part because he has laid out such an effective argument against containment and for disruption, by force, if necessary."

The president's words were widely understood to mean that under no circumstances would Iran be permitted to develop nuclear weapons, even if it took military action—presumably an air and rocket attack against Iran's nuclear facilities—to stop it. Goldberg cautioned, of course, that:

> "it's possible in a second term... he will change his mind... but the record is the record: given the number of times he's told the American public, and the world, that he will stop Iran from going nuclear, it is hard to believe that he will suddenly change his mind and back out of his promise."[23]

But the record shows that he did precisely that after his reelection, and especially after the 2014 midterms: he changed his policy from stopping Iran from obtaining nuclear weapons to *postponing when* Iran would be allowed to develop nuclear weapons. And he conveyed this change to Iranian leadership by dramatically changing his words and his tone with regard to the possible use of military force to stop Iran from amassing a nuclear arsenal. The following chart demonstrates this change.

President Obama's Statements Regarding Iran Nuclear Negotiations & Iran Nuclear Deal

OBAMA'S FIRST TERM[24]

Date	Statement
8 June 2008	"The danger from Iran is grave, it is real, and my goal will be to eliminate this threat. . . . Finally, let there be no doubt: I will always keep the threat of military action on the table to defend our security and our ally Israel."
7 October 2008	"We cannot allow Iran to get a nuclear weapon. It would be a game-changer in the region. Not only would it threaten Israel, our strongest ally in the region and one of our strongest allies in the world, but it would also create a possibility of nuclear weapons falling into the hands of terrorists. And so it's unacceptable. And I will do everything that's required to prevent it. And we will never take military options off the table."
7 November 2008	"Iran's development of a nuclear weapon, I believe, is unacceptable. And we have to mount an international effort to prevent that from happening."
27 January 2010	"And as Iran's leaders continue to ignore their obligations, there should be no doubt: they too will face growing consequences. That is a promise."

1 July 2010

"There should be no doubt—the United States and the international community are determined to prevent Iran from acquiring nuclear weapons."

19 May 2011

"Now, our opposition to Iran's intolerance and Iran's repressive measures, as well as its illicit nuclear program and its support of terror, is well known."

22 May 2011

"You also see our commitment to our shared security in our determination to prevent Iran from acquiring nuclear weapons.... So let me be absolutely clear—we remain committed to preventing Iran from acquiring nuclear weapons."

13 October 2011

"Now, we don't take any options off the table in terms of how we operate with Iran."

14 November 2011

"I have said repeatedly and I will say it today, we are not taking any options off the table, because it's my firm belief that an Iran with a nuclear weapon would pose a security threat not only to the region but also to the United States."

8 December 2011

"No options off the table means I'm considering all options."

16 December 2011

"Another grave concern—and a threat to the security of Israel, the United States and the world—is Iran's nuclear program. And that's why our policy has been absolutely clear: We are determined to prevent Iran from acquiring nuclear weapons... and that's why, rest assured, we will take no options off the table. We have been clear."

24 January 2012

"Let there be no doubt: America is determined to prevent Iran from getting a nuclear weapon, and

I will take no options off the table to achieve that goal."

2 March 2012 "I... don't, as a matter of sound policy, go around advertising exactly what our intentions are. But I think both the Iranian and the Israeli governments recognize that when the United States says it is unacceptable for Iran to have a nuclear weapon, we mean what we say."

4 March 2012 "I have said that when it comes to preventing Iran from obtaining a nuclear weapon, I will take no options off the table, and I mean what I say. That includes all elements of American power: a political effort aimed at isolating Iran; a diplomatic effort to sustain our coalition and ensure that the Iranian program is monitored; an economic effort that imposes crippling sanctions; and, yes, a military effort to be prepared for any contingency."

5 March 2012 "...I reserve all options, and my policy here is not going to be one of containment. My policy is prevention of Iran obtaining nuclear weapons. And as I indicated yesterday in my speech, when I say all options are at the table, I mean it."

6 March 2012 "And what I have said is, is that we will not countenance Iran getting a nuclear weapon. My policy is not containment; my policy is to prevent them from getting a nuclear weapon—because if they get a nuclear weapon that could trigger an arms race in the region, it would undermine our non-proliferation goals, it could potentially fall into the hands of terrorists."

14 March 2012 "...And as I said in a speech just a couple of weeks ago, I am determined not simply to contain

Iran that is in possession of a nuclear weapon; I am determined to prevent Iran from getting a nuclear weapon.... We will do everything we can to resolve this diplomatically, but ultimately, we've got to have somebody on the other side of the table who's taking this seriously."

25 September 2012	"Make no mistake: a nuclear armed Iran is not a challenge that can be contained... the United States will do what we must to prevent Iran from obtaining a nuclear weapon."

Obama's Second Term: Before the Midterm Elections

Date	Statement
14 March 2013[25]	"There is a window, not an infinite period of time, a window of time where we can resolve this diplomatically.... Right now we think that it would take over a year or so for Iran to actually develop a nuclear weapon, but we obviously don't want to cut it too close.... If we can resolve it diplomatically, that's a more lasting solution.... When I say that all options are on the table, all options are on the table. And the US obviously has significant capabilities."
15 March 2013[26]	"I have been crystal clear about my position on Iran possessing a nuclear weapon. That is a red line for us. It is not only something that would be dangerous for Israel. It would be dangerous for the world...."
15 September 2013[27]	I think what the Iranians understand is that—the nuclear issue—is a far larger issue for us than the chemical weapons issue, that—the threat against Iran—against Israel, that a nuclear Iran poses, is much closer to our core interests. That—a nuclear arms race in the region—is something

that would be profoundly destabilizing…. My suspicion is that the Iranians recognize they shouldn't draw a lesson that we haven't struck [Syria] to think we won't strike Iran…."

5 October 2013[28]   "But what I've said to Prime Minister Netanyahu is that the entire point of us setting up sanctions and putting pressure on the Iranian economy was to bring them to the table in a serious way to see if we can resolve this issue diplomatically. And we've got to test that. We're not going to take a bad deal. We are going to make sure that we verify any agreement that we might strike."

23 November 2013[29]   "Since I took office, I've made clear my determination to prevent Iran from obtaining a nuclear weapon. As I've said many times, my strong preference is to resolve this issue peacefully, and we've extended the hand of diplomacy. Yet for many years, Iran has been unwilling to meet its obligations to the international community. So my administration worked with Congress, the United Nations Security Council and countries around the world to impose unprecedented sanctions on the Iranian government…. Today, that diplomacy opened up a new path toward a world that is more secure—a future in which we can verify that Iran's nuclear program is peaceful and that it cannot build a nuclear weapon…. If we can't get there, then no deal is better than a bad deal. But presuming that it's going to be a bad deal, and as a consequence, not even trying for a deal, I think, would be a dire pursuit."

7 December 2013[30]   "The best way for us to prevent Iran from getting a nuclear weapon is for a comprehensive, verifiable, diplomatic resolution, without taking any other options off the table if we fail to achieve that. It is

important for us to test that proposition during the next six months."

27 February 2014[31]	Regarding whether Iran takes the use of military force seriously: "I know they take it seriously... We have a high degree of confidence that when they look at 35,000 US military personnel in the region that are engaged in constant training exercises under the direction of a president who already has shown himself willing to take military action in the past, that they should take my statements seriously."

Obama's Second Term: After the Midterm Elections

Date	*Statement*
9 November 2014[32]	"We have two big interests in Iran that are short term and then we got a long-term interest. Our number one priority with respect to Iran is making sure they don't get [a] nuclear weapon. And because of the unprecedented sanctions that this administration put forward and mobilized the world to abide by, they got squeezed, their economy tanked, and they came to the table in a serious way for the first time in a very, very long time. We've now had significant negotiations. They have abided by freezing their program and, in fact, reducing their stockpile of nuclear-grade material or—or weapons-grade nuclear material. And the question now is are we going to be able to close this final gap so that they can reenter the international community, sanctions can be slowly reduced, and we have verifiable, lock-tight assurances that they can't develop a nuclear weapon."

23 November 2014[33]

"I'm confident that if we reach a deal that is verifiable and ensures that Iran does not have breakout capacity, that not only can I persuade Congress, but I can persuade the American people that it's the right thing to do.... What a deal would do... is take a big piece of business off the table and perhaps begin a long process in which the relationship not just between Iran and us but the relationship between Iran and the world, and the region, begins to change.... I think Iran would love to see the sanctions end immediately, and then to still have some avenues that might not be completely closed, and we can't do that."

29 December 2014[34]

"Having said that, if we can get a deal on making sure that Iran does not have a nuclear weapon—and that deal is possible; we know the terms of what that would look like. If Iran recognizes that it is in its own interests, having already said that they're actually not interested in developing a nuclear weapon, to go ahead and prove that to the world, so that over time as it's verified, sanctions are removed, their economy begins to grow, they're reintegrated into the international community—if we can take that big first step, then my hope would be that that would serve as the basis for us trying to improve relations over time.... If you look at the negotiations as they've proceeded, what we've said to the Iranians is that we are willing to recognize your ability to develop a modest nuclear power program for your energy needs—that there's a way of doing that that nevertheless gives the world assurances that you don't have breakout capacity."

2 March 2015[35]

"If, in fact, Iran is willing to agree to double-digit years of keeping their program where it is right now and, in fact, rolling back elements of it that currently exist... if we've got that, and we've got a way of verifying that, there's no other steps we can take that would give us such assurance that they don't have a nuclear weapon."

7 April 2015[36]

"My goal, when I first came into office, was to make sure that Iran did not get a nuclear weapon and thereby trigger a nuclear arms race in the most volatile part of the world.... We're now in a position where Iran has agreed to unprecedented inspections and verifications of its program, providing assurances that it is peaceful in nature.... Currently, the breakout times [for Iran to complete a nuclear weapon] are only about two to three months by our intelligence estimates. So essentially, we're purchasing for 13, 14, 15 years assurances that the breakout is at least a year..."

1 June 2015[37]

"I can, I think, demonstrate, not based on any hope but on facts and evidence and analysis, that the best way to prevent Iran from having a nuclear weapon is a verifiable tough agreement. A military solution will not fix it. Even if the United States will participates, it would temporarily slow down an Iranian nuclear program, but it will not eliminate it...."

14 July 2015[38]

"We're not measuring this deal by whether we are solving every problem that can be traced back to Iran, whether we are eliminating all their nefarious activities around the globe. We are measuring this deal—and that was the original premise of this conversation, including by Prime Minister Netanyahu—Iran could not get a nuclear weapon. That was always the discussion.

> And what I'm going to be able to say, and I think
> we will be able to prove, is that this by a wide
> margin is the most definitive path by which Iran
> will not get a nuclear weapon, and we will be able
> to achieve that with the full cooperation of the
> world community and without having to engage
> in another war in the Middle East."

President Obama's statement of 1 June 2015 that "a military
solution will not fix it [but would only] temporarily slow down
an Iranian nuclear program... not eliminate it," sent a clear message to Iranian leaders that they had little to fear from a military
option and that they could now negotiate as equals. This message was reiterated at various points by administration and state
department officials as well.*

When President Obama invited me to discuss Iran in the Oval
Office just prior to his second election, he looked me straight in

---

* See Anne-Marie Slaughter (formerly of the State Department): "I
don't know any security expert who is recommending a military strike
on Iran at this point...", W. Patrick Lang (formerly of the Defense
Intelligence Agency): "Unless you're so far over on the neocon side
that you're blind to geopolitical realities, there's an overwhelming consensus that this [attacking Iran] is a bad idea...", and Michele Flournoy
(formerly of the Department of Defense): "Most security experts agree
that it's premature to go to the military option...." Nicholas Kristof,
"The False Debate About Attacking Iran," *New York Times*, 24 March
2012; Michael Hayden also said: "when we talked about this in the
government, the consensus was that [attacking Iran] would guarantee
that which we are trying to prevent—an Iran that will spare nothing to
build a nuclear weapon and that would build it in secret..." at an event
at the Center for the National Interest according to Josh Rogin, "Bush's
CIA Director: We Determined Attacking Iran Was a Bad Idea," *Foreign
Policy*, 19 January 2012; see also Stephen M. Walt, "Why Attacking Iran
is Still a Bad Idea," *Foreign Policy*, 27 December 2011.

the eye and assured me that the military option was on the table and that Iran would not be allowed to develop a nuclear weapon "whatever it takes." I certainly took him at his word. The question I now ask myself is whether President Obama changed his mind following his reelection or whether he was always bluffing about the military option. It now seems likely that Obama never really considered seriously any military option. The very fact that he has set out the only realistic alternative to a deal as Iran developing a nuclear weapon more quickly, strongly suggests that he has never really considered preventing Iran from developing nuclear weapons by the use, or credible threat, of military means.

If Obama really still had the military option on the table when the negotiations were beginning, it would seem to follow that he subsequently made a decision to take it off the table. That is certainly how the Iranians perceived it. As Ayatollah Ali Khamenei recently put it: "Negotiation under the ghost of a threat is meaningless," because America "can't do a damn thing."[39] Even one Israeli former intelligence official who believes the deal is better than no deal, Admiral Ami Ayalon, has criticized President Obama's negotiation strategy: "[He] doesn't have the right combination of the language of peace and the language of war. He has to make it very clear that while he believes in diplomacy, he also knows how to use force."[40] But following his reelection and the midterm results, President Obama used the wrong combination of language, which led the Iranian leadership to believe that the US would not take military action if there was no deal.

The end result of the negotiations is that the US now has no military options unless the Iranians cheat in a provocative way, and even then it is doubtful that Obama would now employ a military force. Israel, which is not bound by the deal because it was not allowed to participate in the negotiations, still has military options, but Israel is far less likely to be able to employ them, since the international community stands behind the deal. Russia is preparing to send Iran a sophisticated missile defense system,[41] and the deal itself encourages members of the P5 plus one to help Iran securitize its nuclear program.[42] Secretary of State Kerry has warned that an Israeli attack on Iran's nuclear program would be a "huge mistake."[43] So under this deal, Iran has succeeded in reducing, if not eliminating, the threat of military action, ending the crippling sanctions, and changing its status from that of a lawless pariah nation to that of an equal partner in negotiations. As Thomas L. Friedman aptly put it in his article of 22 July 2015: "The balance of power became too equal."

What has the international community received in return? That remains to be seen. But if it is only a short-term moratorium on Iran's nuclear weapons program, the negotiations can hardly be considered the success that President Obama claims they are.

If I am correct, then President Obama should be judged harshly, not necessarily for accepting a deal that may (or may not) be less bad than the alternative of rejecting it, but rather for allowing us to be presented with only two alternative outcomes, neither of which is particularly good for the world, for America, and for our Middle East allies. We could have gotten a better deal had Obama kept his pre-reelection promise of preventing Iran from developing nuclear weapons "whatever it takes," including the threatened use of military force as a last resort, if the Iranians refused to accept our original red lines and if they moved toward the nuclear threshold.

An analogy comes to mind from my own experience as a criminal lawyer who has negotiated many deals on behalf of clients accused of serious crimes. In engaging in plea bargaining, it is important to maintain a credible threat to go to trial and possibly win an acquittal if an acceptable plea bargain is not approved by the prosecution. I've seen many mediocre criminal lawyers accept a deal that, while better than the alternative, was far worse than what a good lawyer could have achieved. Consider the following realistic situation. A good lawyer represents a white collar defendant charged with stock fraud. Were he to be convicted, he would receive a sentence of ten years under the guidelines. Because the prosecutor fears that this good lawyer might actually secure an acquittal were he to go to trial, he is willing to accept a plea that would result in a three-year sentence. A mediocre lawyer, who presents no credible threat of going to trial and winning, might not be able to do *better* than a seven-year prison deal. That seven-year deal is better than the ten years the defendant would have gotten had he been convicted. But it is considerably worse than the three-year sentence the good lawyer obtained for his client. If the bad lawyer asked to be judged "on one thing"—is the deal he secured for his client "a better outcome... than any other alternatives on the table?"[44]—he would be judged positively, as Obama wishes to be judged. But if he is to be judged on whether *he* got the best deal possible, he would be judged harshly, as President Obama deserves to be judged by putting us in the position of accepting a deal that is not as good as we could have gotten had he kept a credible military threat on the table—even if the current deal is better than the alternative.

Putting aside the important past question of whether we could have done better, the current question is whether the alternative to accepting this deal is actually worse than accepting it. I will address that question in the pages to come. The answer to that broad policy question may turn on the answers to a series of subquestions such as following:

First, what does the deal itself contemplate? Is it a relatively short moratorium designed to manage the Iranian nuclear program or a relatively long prohibition on Iran developing a nuclear arsenal? What is the position of the US on this question? The rest of the P5 plus one? Iran?

Second, even if the terms of the deal themselves are acceptable, can the Iranians be trusted not to try to evade its constraints?

Third, if they cannot be trusted—which all reasonable people must assume—are there effective verification methods in place capable of immediately detecting any cheating?

Fourth, if the Iranians are caught cheating, will there be consequences, and if so what will they be? Would the military option be placed back on the table?

Fifth, what if the Iranians comply with the terms of the deal but use the hundreds of billions of dollars they will received from the sanction relief to purchase and distribute to their surrogates massive amounts of sophisticated nonnuclear weapons and increase their export of terrorism and their hegemonic aggression on the region?

These are important variables, but the two constants are that, despite their claims to the contrary, Iran is determined to assemble a nuclear arsenal as soon as possible, and that Iran wants all economic sanctions to end as quickly as possible. These two constants *should* be in direct conflict with each other, *unless* the deal eliminates or minimizes the conflict by quickly ending the sanctions while merely delaying briefly Iran's progress on nuclear weapons. That was Iran's goal in negotiating the deal and it remains Iran's goal as the deal is implemented. America's goal was to implement its controversial world view about its place in the international community and the role of negotiation in resolving conflicts. President Obama is genuinely concerned about a nuclear Iran, but he seems willing, in the words of *New York Times* analyst David E. Sanger, to "roll the dice" and place a "bet" on his "faith" that the deal will change the behavior of the Iranians.[45]

The chapters to come will address the questions—in roughly chronological order—of how we got to where we are now, whether this is a good or bad bet, whether it is appropriate for a superpower like the US to roll dice or rely on faith and questionable wagers when the stakes are so high, whether it would be worse now to reject this deal and live with the consequences, and whether there are viable alternatives—or additions—to simply accepting or rejecting the deal.

President Obama has accused critics of his deal of being the same Republican warmongers who drove us into the ground war against Iraq, and said that they would offer "overheated and often dishonest argument."[46] I am a liberal democrat who twice supported President Obama's elections and opposed the war in Iraq. My goal in this book is to offer a rational nuanced and honest assessment of how we got to where we are and the upsides and downsides of the current deal. And there are both upsides and downsides. Depending on its interpretation and implementation, this deal may not be as good as its most enthusiastic proponents claim, nor as bad as its harshest critics fear.* It is for the public to judge the persuasiveness and credibility of the arguments on all sides and to decide whether, on balance, this is a good or bad deal on its own merits, and whether it is better—or less worse—than its alternatives.

---

* A man who I deeply admire—Israel's former Mossad head Efraim Halevy—has characterized the deal as "not entirely bad" and has said that it will take time to judge whether it is good or bad overall. Ben Caspit, "We Have All Lost," *Jerusalem Post*, 17 July 2015.

In the conclusion of this book, I offer a constructive alternative to Congress simply accepting or rejecting this deal. I propose veto-proof legislation that will considerably increase the odds that Iran will stand by its reaffirmation in the words of the deal, that it will not "ever," under any circumstances, "seek, develop, or acquire any nuclear weapons."

Alan Dershowitz
New York, NY
August 2015

PART I.
MAINTAINING MILITARY OPTIONS

I HAVE ALWAYS BELIEVED, *and still believe, that the only way to get a tyrannical and aggressive regime like Iran to end its nuclear weapons program is by the credible threat of military action coupled with crippling economic pressure. The difference between these two threats is that the United States alone is capable of conveying a military threat, whereas it takes collective action by the world's most powerful economies—including China, Russia, and Western Europe—to threaten to produce and maintain a crippling economic sanctions regime.*

For that reason, the United States should have announced at the beginning of the nuclear negotiations a bright red line: the United States will never allow Iran to develop a nuclear weapons program. That should have been the constant, about which Iran had no say and about which there would be no negotiations. The variables would be how we achieve that constant: whether through negotiations, sanctions or—as a last resort—surgical military attack, repeated when and if Iran were to start its nuclear program again. Economic suffering alone would never drive a fundamentalist regime into submission. But crippling sanctions, coupled with the realization that we would never allow them to develop nuclear weapons, would have put us in a strong position from which to negotiate. Unilaterally giving up this advantage weakened our bargaining position considerably.

As we shall see in the chapters that come, I have taken this position from the beginning. And so did the Obama administration—at least in its early rhetoric. As we shall also see, the credibility of that option diminished over time, thus weakening our bargaining position.

The first part of this book sets out the legal, moral, military, political, and pragmatic case for maintaining a strong military option—coupled with the hope and desire that it would never have to be deployed.

In 2006, I wrote two articles on the military option against the Iranian nuclear weapons program. The first, which was published as a chapter in an academic book entitled Preemption: A Knife that Cuts Both Ways, *set out the options available to stop Iran's nuclear weapons program as well as the legal and moral considerations relevant to a possible preemptive or preventive military attack against Iran's nuclear weapons program. The second, which appeared in the British magazine* The Spectator, *dealt with the practical limitations on any military actions.*

A. *The Options for Preventing Iran from Developing Nuclear Weapons*[47]

This chapter consists of a case study of the options regarding Iran's nuclear program. No reasonable person can doubt that the Iranian government wants to develop a nuclear weapon capacity. Despite its claim that it is seeking only to expand its energy sources, the evidence to the contrary is significant, if not overwhelming. First, Iran has enormous oil reserves and access to other nonnuclear sources of energy. Second, the material Iran is trying to import is of the type necessary for the construction of nuclear weapons, not merely nuclear energy. Third, several prominent Iranian politicians have acknowledged the military goals of the nuclear program. President Mohammad Khatami has threatened to use Iran's missiles to destroy Jewish and Christian civilization!

> "Our missiles are now ready to strike at their civilization, and as soon as the instructions arrive from the leader, Ali Khamenei, we will launch our missiles at their cities and installations."[48]

Khamenei has in turn urged his military to "have two [nuclear] bombs ready to go in January [2005] or you are not Muslims."[49] On 21 September 2004 the Iranian military paraded its Shahab-3 missile through the streets of Tehran. These missiles, which can reach Israeli and Iraqi cities, were draped with banners that read "Crush America" and "Wipe Israel Off the Map."[50] In late October 2004, shouts of "Death to America" followed the rejection by the Iranian "legislature" of a proposal to assure peaceful use of nuclear technology. And in May of 2005, it was disclosed that Iran had converted thirty-seven tons of uranium into gas, which "could theoretically yield more than 200 pounds of weapons-grade uranium, enough to make five crude nuclear weapons."[51] Several days later, Prime Minister Tony Blair of Britain warned that he was prepared to seek sanctions from the UN Security Council if Iran proceeded with plans to resume uranium reprocessing.[52] The foreign ministers of Britain, France, and Germany wrote a sharply worded letter warning that any attempt to restart Iran's nuclear program "would bring the negotiating process to an end." But Iran responded defiantly that it "will definitely resume a part of its enrichment activities in the near future."[53]

This apocalyptic attitude, combined with an expectation of heavenly reward for killing millions of Jews and Americans, makes the effectiveness of the usual deterrent approach to nuclear threat somewhat less promising than if directed against a more secular regime. Some Muslim extremists—whether they be conventional suicide bombers or nuclear suicide bombers— will not be deterred by the threat of mere death, and certainly not by sanctions. They welcome martyrdom as a necessary prelude to a paradise in which they will be rewarded for their martyrdom. This does not mean, of course, that a credible threat of material or economic damage will necessarily be ignored by all of those in power. There are pragmatists and materialists even among the most fundamentalist zealots. Moreover, there are genuine moderates and reformers both inside and outside the Iranian government, and their potential impact on Iranian nuclear policy cannot be overlooked. But in any worst-case scenario—a scenario that also cannot be ignored especially by the potentially targeted state—the threatening statements made by those in power must be given considerable weight.

Estimates vary as to the timing of Iran's independent development of deliverable nuclear weapons. Some believe it is as far as three to five years away—if it does not receive outside help.* As one retired CIA official has put it:

> The big wild card for us is that you don't know who is capable of filling in the missing parts for them... North Korea? Pakistan? We don't know what parts are missing."[54]

What is clear is that "its work on a missile-delivery system is far more advanced"[55] and that it has plans to arm its missiles with nuclear, chemical, and/or biological warheads capable of mass destruction and murder of millions of civilians. Whether there are those in positions of authority who are actually contemplating the suicidal deployment of such weapons is, of course, far less clear, though the events of 9/11 made nothing unthinkable.

No democracy can afford to wait until such a threat against its civilian population is imminent. Both Israel and the United States should have the right, under international law, to protect their civilians and soldiers from a threatened nuclear holocaust, and that right must include—if that is the only realistic

---

* At the time, the five-5year estimate was widely circulated; see for example Greg Jones, "When Could Iran Have the Bomb? An Analysis of Recent Statements that Iran Is 3 to 5 Years Away," *Non-Proliferation Policy Education Center*, 27 April 2010.

option—preemptive military action of the sort taken by Israel against the Iraqi nuclear reactor at Osirak in 1981, especially if such action can again be taken without an unreasonable number of civilian casualties.

Although the Security Council of the UN unanimously voted to condemn Israel's attack on the Iraqi reactor, [former] Secretary of State Condoleezza Rice has said that history had vindicated the Israeli strike by preventing Saddam Hussein from gaining access to nuclear weapons, but she declined to say whether the United States would support an Osirak-type attack by Israel against Iranian nuclear facilities. No two situations are ever exactly the same, and the considerations that must go into any military decision will depend on many subtle factors. Secretary Rice did say, however, that the United States and its allies "cannot allow the Iranians to develop a nuclear weapon."[56] That appears to be the *constant* in the equation, with the *variable* being the *means* that might appropriately be employed to assure that neither the United States nor its allies will have to confront an Iran with a nuclear weapon capability (as we may already be facing a North Korea with such capability).

There have been periodic reports suggesting that the United States may be selling bunker-busting bombs to Israel, weapons that could be used to destroy the underground nuclear facilities being used by Iran to protect its nuclear weapons work-in-progress.[57] Whether this information was leaked in order to bolster the deterrence threat or to enhance Israel's actual capacity to destroy the Iranian nuclear facilities is unknown.

Despite statements about the propriety of Israel's attack against the Iraqi nuclear reactor and the unacceptability of Iran developing a nuclear bomb, the American policy with regard to the Iranian nuclear program remains unclear. The former under secretary of defense for policy has said that "I don't think that anyone should be ruling in or out anything while we are conducting diplomacy,"[58] but the president [Bush] has not spoken directly about the military issue. To the contrary, he has said that "diplomacy must be the first choice, and always the first choice of an administration trying to solve an issue of... nuclear armament. And we'll continue to press on diplomacy."[59] That is certainly the correct view in any situation in which there is a heavy burden on those contemplating a military option. Former president Bill Clinton commended President Bush for keeping "the military option on the table, but not pushing it too far."[60] But the question remains: If all diplomatic options fail, as they did with regard to Iraq in 1981, must a democratic nation committed to the rule of law as well as to its own survival and the protection of its citizens wait for help from an unfriendly Security Council (some of whose members have supplied Iran with the materials it may now be using to build nuclear weapons), or may it—as a last resort—take preventive military action, as Israel did in 1981?

Today most reasonable people look to Israel's surgical attack against the Osirak nuclear reactor as the paradigm of proportional preemption, despite the Security Council's condemnation. (Many forget that Iran actually attacked the Iraqi reactor before Israel did, but failed to destroy it; there was no UN condemnation of *that* attack.) If the Iranian nuclear facilities were all located in one place, away from any civilian population center, it would be moral (and under any reasonable regime of international law, legal) for Israel or the United States to destroy it if all nonmilitary options failed. But the Iranian militants have learned from the Iraqi experience and, according to intelligence reports, have deliberately spread their nuclear facilities around the country, including in or near heavily populated areas. This could force Israel or the US into a terrible choice: either allow Iran to complete its production of nuclear bombs aimed at its own civilian population centers and other targets, or destroy the facilities despite the inevitability of Iranian civilian casualties. The longer they wait, the greater the risks to civilians, especially if they wait until an attack on the reactors might spread radiation.

The laws of war prohibit the bombing of civilian population centers (even in retaliation for or deterrence of attacks on cities) but they permit the bombing of military targets, including nuclear facilities during wartime.[61] By deliberately placing nuclear facilities in the midst of civilian population centers, the Iranian government has made the decision to expose its civilians to attacks, and it must assume all responsibility for any casualties caused by such attacks. In the context of domestic law, when a criminal uses an innocent bystander as a "shield" against the police, and the police, in a reasonable effort to apprehend the criminal, unintentionally shoot and kill the innocent shield, it is the criminal who is guilty of murder, even though the policeman fired the fatal shot.* The same rule of culpability should apply in the military context. Israel, the United States, and other democracies locate their military facilities away from population centers, precisely in order to minimize danger to their civilians.

---

*   Federal law states that "whoever… seizes or detains and threatens to kill, to injure, or to continue to detain another person in order to compel a third person or a governmental organization to do or abstain from doing any act as an explicit or implicit condition for the release of the person detained… shall be punished by imprisonment for any term of years or for life and, if the death of any person results, shall be punished by death or life imprisonment." 18 USC. 1203. The law does not specify who must have caused the death; if someone dies, the hostage taker is responsible.

Iran does precisely the opposite, because its leaders realize that decent democracies would hesitate to bomb a nuclear facility located in an urban center.* They use their own civilians as a deterrent against a preventive attack.

Israel (with the help of the United States) should try everything short of military action first—diplomacy, threats, bribery, sabotage, targeted killings of individuals essential to the Iranian nuclear program, and other covert actions. But if all else fails, Israel (or the United States) must have the option of taking out the Iranian nuclear threat before it is capable of the genocide for which its leaders assert it is being built. The Chief of Staff of the Israeli Defense Forces put it this way:

> "We believe there is a chance of success when talking about the elimination of the Iranian capabilities of weapons of mass destruction, first of all using political and economic resolutions, from my point of view and my recommendation, this has to be used first of all. If not we have to be prepared, and I am talking about the Western community, to use other options in order to eliminate the Iranian capabilities."[62]

In June of 2004, it was reported that:

> Israel already had rehearsed a military first strike on Iran. "Israel will on no account permit Iranian

---

* Menachem Begin said, in explaining the timing of the Osirak attack: "[I]f the reactor had become... hot, we couldn't do anything further. Because if... we would open it... a horrifying wave of radioactivity would come out from the reactor and cover the sky over Baghdad... Hundreds of thousands of innocent citizens—residents, men, women, and children—would have been hurt." Shlomo Nakdimon, *First Strike: The Exclusive Story of How Israel Foiled Iraq's Attempt to Get the Bomb,* (New York: Summit, 1987) p. 239.

reactors—especially the one being built in Bushehr with Russian help—to go critical," an Israeli defense source told reporters. Prime Minister Ariel Sharon went on the record that Iran was the "biggest danger to the existence of Israel." Sharon left no doubt as to his meaning: "Israel will not allow Iran to be equipped with a nuclear weapon."[63]

In early 2005, Israel's foreign minister, Silvan Shalom, reiterated the point that if European diplomatic efforts fail, "Israel cannot live with Iran having a nuclear bomb."[64] Again, that appears to be the constant, with the variables dependent on the success of international diplomacy, sanctions, or other forms of intervention. It is possible, of course, that neither Israel nor the United States has any current fixed intention to attack preventively Iran's nuclear facilities, but are issuing their tough statements as part of an overall deterrent strategy.

According to an article in the 24 January 2005 issue of the *New Yorker* by Seymour Hersh, the US is preparing for the *possibility* of a preemptive military attack against Iran's nuclear weapons program:

> The Administration has been conducting secret reconnaissance missions inside Iran at least since last summer. Much of the focus is on the accumulation of intelligence and targeting information on Iranian nuclear, chemical, and missile sites, both declared and suspected. The goal is to identify and isolate three dozen, and perhaps more, such targets that could be destroyed by precision strikes and short-term commando raids. "The civilians in the Pentagon want to go into Iran and destroy as much of the military infrastructure as possible," the government consultant with close ties to the Pentagon told me.

According to this report, the United States has been confer-
ring with Israel about a possible military preemption:

> There has also been close, and largely unacknowl-
> edged, cooperation with Israel….(After Osirak, Iran
> situated many of its nuclear sites in remote areas of
> the east, in an attempt to keep them out of striking
> range of other countries, especially Israel. Distance
> no longer lends such protection, however: Israel
> has acquired three submarines capable of launching
> cruise missiles and has equipped some of its air-
> craft with additional fuel tanks, putting Israeli F-16I
> fighters within the range of most Iranian targets.)
>
> They believe that about three-quarters of the
> potential targets can be destroyed from the air, and a
> quarter are too close to population centers, or buried
> too deep, to be targeted….

But there are some who doubt the benefits of a military
approach:

> …Shahram Chubin, an Iranian scholar who is the
> director of research at the Geneva Centre for Security
> Policy, told me, "It's a fantasy to think that there's a
> good American or Israeli military option in Iran."
> He went on, "The Israeli view is that this is an inter-
> national problem. 'You do it,' they say to the West.
> 'Otherwise, our Air Force will take care of it.'" …But
> the situation now is both more complex and more
> dangerous [than it was in Iraq in 1981], Chubin said.
> The Osirak bombing "drove the Iranian nuclear weap-
> ons program underground, to hardened, dispersed
> sites," he said. "…The US and Israel would not be cer-
> tain whether all the sites had been hit, or how quickly
> they'd be rebuilt. Meanwhile, they'd be waiting for
> an Iranian counterattack that could be military or

terrorist or diplomatic. Iran has long-range missiles
and ties to Hezbollah, which has drones—you can't
begin to think of what they'd do in response."[65]

In January of 2005, I asked a former very high-ranking Israeli intelligence official whether an Osirak-type preemptive attack was feasible against the Iranian nuclear program. He told me that any such attack would have to be very different from the singular, surgical air attack of 1981. "It would be more difficult, because it would have to be multifaceted. If it were to be carried out, it would be something unprecedented in military history." He also told me that "Israel should not bear the burden alone, because the development of an Iranian nuclear rocket would endanger many other countries as well." He said that the US would be particularly vulnerable to nuclear terrorism if an Iranian nuclear bomb found its way into the hands of Islamic terrorists.

The issue is made even more complex by the internal dynamics of Iranian society, which is deeply divided between the religious zealots now in control and a secular (or at least somewhat more secular) minority (or majority, no one really knows). *New York Times* columnist Thomas L. Friedman reports that if a free and fair election were held in Iran, it might go against what many Iranians regard as the current despotic leadership.* The problem is that, according to some experts, there is no division within Iran as to its right to develop nuclear weapons:

> "The nuclear ambition in Iran is supported across the
> political spectrum, and Iranians will perceive attacks
> on these sites as attacks on their ambitions to be a

---

* Such predictions proved optimistic: the autocratic and ultraconserva-
tive Mahmoud Ahmadinejad was reelected to a second term as Iran's
prime minister in 2009.

major regional player and a modern nation that's tech-
nologically sophisticated."[66]

Two Iranian human rights activists have argued that "for
human rights defenders in Iran, the possibility of a foreign
military attack on that country [by the United States or Israel]
represents an utter disaster for their cause." They worry that
"the threat of foreign military intervention will provide a powerful excuse for authoritarian elements to uproot these [nascent
human rights groups] and put an end to their growth." But they
neglect entirely the threat posed by a nuclear Iran. Demanding
that Israel and the United States put the human rights of Iranians
ahead of the lives of their own citizens and soldiers is both naive
and selfish—unless the unexpressed assumption is that if human
rights were to become strengthened in Iran, the threat of nuclear
weapons would diminish, as it almost certainly would. But the
likelihood that the human rights movement would become
strong enough soon enough to eliminate the nuclear threat is
very slight. I put this question to Israeli Knesset member Natan
Sharansky when he spoke at the Harvard Kennedy School in
February 2005. Sharansky had made a strong case that democracies do not attack other democracies and that the best long-term
approach to Iran is to help strengthen their human rights movements. He also believes that the current leadership of Iran is
determined to develop and use nuclear weapons against Israel,
and he seems to agree with the Iranian human rights activists
that a foreign attack might weaken the human rights movement.
Much will depend on timing: How quickly will the mullahs get
their nuclear bomb? How quickly will the dissidents increase
their influence?

Moreover, an Israeli planner has told me that in light of the
endemic instability in Iran, they would not tolerate nuclear

weapons in that country even if moderates, with no intention of using them aggressively, were to assume control. "Moderate control is temporary, but nuclear weapons in Iran would be permanent," the Israeli planner said. In addition, there is always the risk that Iranian nuclear weapons could fall into the hands of Hezbollah or other terrorists who work closely with Iranians. The Israeli position, as well as the American view, still seems to be that regardless of the internal dynamics of Iranian politics, the constant remains that no nuclear weapons will be tolerated, regardless of who is in charge.

Thus the likelihood that this issue will be resolved internally as slim at best, but internal dynamics should not be ignored. If there were to be an internally generated (or mostly internally generated) regime change within Iran, that might not diminish the government's *desire* to become a nuclear power, but it could diminish the *dangers* posed by its access to nuclear weapons. A more secular, democratic regime—or one less belligerent toward the US (and thus possibly toward Israel)—might be more tolerable to the US and Israel than the suicidal religious extremists who would currently control any nuclear weapons developed or obtained by Iran. A new regime might also pose a smaller risk of having such weapons fall into the hands of terrorists, but it would not eliminate all the risks.[*]

---

*   The *New York Times* reported that the discovery of blueprints for an atomic bomb in the files of the Libyan weapons program "gave the experts a new appreciation of the audacity of the rogue nuclear network led by A.Q. Khan, a chief architect of Pakistan's bomb. The report quotes 'one American expert': 'expert": this was the first time we had ever seen a loose copy of a bomb design that clearly worked, and the question was: Who Else had it? The Iranians? The Syrians?…'

There are, of course, no guarantees, and all of this is a matter of degree and probability. But the risks of a preemptive attack are so considerable that these probabilities and subtle matters of degree must be factored into any calculation of the costs and benefits of every available option. Even if the US and/or Israel have the legal and moral *right* to act preemptively against the development of an Iranian nuclear weapon, it does not necessarily follow that they should *exercise* that right by means of a difficult and risky military strike that might set back any nascent reform movement by uniting all (or most) Iranians against the external threats posed by the United States and Israel.

There are some, however, who argue the opposite: that the destruction of the Iranian nuclear capacity would weaken the mullahs and strengthen the hands of dissidents. No one can be certain what the effects of a successful or failed preemptive attack would be, except that the law of unintended consequences would rear its always unpredictable and often ugly head.

As of now, it is unclear whether the United Nations, the International Atomic Energy Agency, the European Community, or anyone else is actually making progress in stopping the Iranian nuclear weapons program. The Iranian program has been assisted by several nations, including France, Germany, Russia, and Pakistan. Several of these countries, which have profited enormously from doing dirty business with Iran, seem less than anxious for a confrontation with their trading partner. Diplomacy appears to be delaying certain aspects of the program, but for how long no one can be certain. American indecision—a *New York Times* headline of 21 September 2004 read "Bush Aides

---

William J. Broad and David E. Sanger, "As Nuclear Secrets Emerge, More Are Suspected," *New York Times*, 26 December 2004, p. 21.

Divided on Confronting Iran Over A-Bomb"[67]—seems to be
encouraging the Iranians to speed up their program, so as to be
able to deter a preemptive strike by threatening a counterstrike
with nuclear weapons. During the presidential election campaign of 2004, Hassan Rohani, the head of the Iranian Supreme
National Security Council, said he was hoping that President
Bush would be reelected because the Bush administration was
doing little to prevent Iran from developing its nuclear program.
He said that despite President Bush's "hard-line and baseless
rhetoric," the president has not taken "in practical terms" any
"dangerous actions" against the mullahs or their nuclear program.[68] Perhaps the disclosures regarding pentagon planning for
a possible attack were intended to counter this perception and
to increase the pressure on Iran. The situation may soon reach
crisis proportions. Yet there is certainly no consensus among
international law scholars about the legality, propriety, morality,
or wisdom of a preventive attack on Iran's nuclear facilities. There
is not even consensus about the factors that should be considered in making such a decision.

Were the nightmare scenarios of a nuclear mass casualty attack
by Iran (or a terrorist surrogate like Hezbollah) to occur because
of the failure to act by nations capable of preventatively destroying Iran's nuclear capacity, we may someday hear an Iranian mass
murderer echo Goebbels's bewilderment about why the World
War I victors had not prevented Nazi Germany from arming.[69]
In retrospect, the bewilderment expressed by Goebbels sounds
like an apt warning, but in prospect—without any certain knowledge how the Iranian situation will play out—it is only one of
many historical lessons from which to learn.

In the end, any decision with regard to the Iranian nuclear
program will probably be based less on international law than on

the practical military capacity of those nations most at risk—the US and Israel—to destroy the Iranian reactors without undue civilian casualties and other costs. It will also depend on whether the international community demonstrates a capacity to confront threats of this kind by collective action.

B. *The Difficulties of Deploying Military Actions against Iran*[70]

Face it. Iran probably will get the bomb. It has already test-fired rockets capable of targeting the entire Middle East and much of southern Europe. And it claims to have 40,000 suicide volunteers eager to deploy terrorism—even nuclear terrorism—against its enemies. With a nuclear capacity, the Islamic Republic of Iran will instantly achieve the status of superpower to which Iraq aspired.

Nothing currently on the table will deter Iran. Sanctions are paper protests to an oil-rich nation. Diplomacy has already failed because Russia and China are playing both sides. Sabotage, bribery—even assassination of nuclear scientists—may delay but will not prevent Iran from becoming a nuclear power. That leaves military threats and, ultimately, military action.

First, consider military threats. They are already coming from two sources: the US and Israel. Neither is working, for very different reasons.

The Iranians would probably give up their nuclear weapons program if their leaders truly believed that refusal to do so would produce an Iraq-like attack—an all-out invasion, regime change, and occupation. Leaders, even religious leaders, fear imprisonment and death. Only the United States is capable of mounting such a sustained attack.

But the continuing war in Iraq has made it impossible for the US to mount a credible threat, because American public opinion would not accept a second war—or so the Iranians believe. Moreover, America's allies in the war against Iraq—most particularly Great Britain—would not support an attack on Iran.

That is precisely why the Bush administration is barking so loudly. It wants to convince the Iranian leadership that it is preparing to bite—to attack, invade, and destroy their regime, perhaps even with the use of tactical nuclear weapons. But it's not working. It is only causing the Iranian leaders themselves to bark louder, to exaggerate their progress toward completing a nuclear weapon and to threaten terrorist retaliation by its suicide volunteers if Iran were to be attacked.

The war in Iraq is a two-edged sword when it comes to Iran. One edge demonstrates that the US is willing and able to topple dictatorial regimes that it regards as dangerous. That is the edge the Bush administration is trying to showcase. The other edge represents the failure of Iraq—widespread public distrust of intelligence claims, fear of becoming bogged down in another endless war, strident opposition at home and abroad. That is the edge being seen by the Iranian leaders. The US threat is seen as hollow.

That leaves the Israeli threat, which is real but limited. Who could blame Israel for seeking to destroy the emerging nuclear capacity of an enemy nation whose leader, as recently as 14 April 2006, threatened to eliminate 'the Zionist regime' by 'one storm'—a clear reference to a nuclear attack.

These threats of a nuclear attack are being taken seriously by Israeli leaders, even if they are neither imminent nor certain.

Israelis remember apocalyptic threats from an earlier dictator that were not taken seriously. This time those threatened have the military capacity to confront the danger and are likely to do so if it becomes more likely. Even if Israelis believe there is only a 5 percent chance that Iran would attack Israel with nuclear weapons, the risk of national annihilation would be too great for any nation—and most especially one built on the ashes of the Holocaust—to ignore.

The Iranian leaders understand this. They take seriously the statements made by Israeli leaders that they will never accept a nuclear Iran under its present leadership. They fully expect an attack from Israel when they come close to producing a nuclear weapon. Why then are they not deterred by the realistic prospect of an Israeli preemptive (or preventive) strike? For three related reasons. First, an Israeli attack would be a limited, surgical strike (or series of strikes). It would not be accompanied by a full-scale invasion, occupation, and regime change. Second, it would only delay production of a nuclear bomb, because it would be incomplete. Some nuclear facilities would be missed or only damaged, because they are 'hardened' and/or located in populated areas. The third and most important reason is that an attack by Israel would solidify the Iranian regime. It would make Iran into the victim of 'Zionist aggression' and unify Muslims, both inside and outside of Iran, against their common enemies. I say enemies because regardless of what role the US played or did not play in an Israeli attack, the US would share the blame in the radical Islamic world.

I am not going so far as to argue that the Iranian leadership would welcome an Israeli attack, but it would quickly turn such an attack to its advantage. If matters get worse domestically for the Iranian regime—if the nascent anti-Ahmadinejad 'democratic' or 'secular' movements were to strengthen—Ahmadinejad might actually get to the point of welcoming, even provoking or faking, an attack from Israel. This is why the threat from Israel will not work as a deterrent.

So we have two threats: one from a superpower—the US—that can but won't bring about regime change. The other from a regional power—Israel—that may well attack but, if it does, will not only fail to produce regime change, but may actually strengthen the existing regime.

The Iranians will persist therefore in their efforts to secure nuclear weapons. Unless they are stopped or significantly delayed by military actions, they will become a nuclear power within a few years—precisely how many is unknown and probably unknowable. Armed with nuclear weapons and ruled by religious fanatics, Iran will become the most dangerous nation in the world. There is a small but still real possibility that it could initiate a suicidal nuclear exchange with Israel. There is a far greater likelihood that it could hand over nuclear material to one of its terrorist surrogates or that some rogue elements could steal nuclear material. This would pose a direct threat to the United States and all its allies.

The world should not accept these risks if there are reasonable steps available to prevent or reduce them. The question remains: Are any such steps feasible? Probably not, as long as the US remains bogged down in Iraq. History may well conclude that America and Britain fought the wrong preventive war against a country that posed no real threat, and that fighting that wrong war stopped them from fighting the right preventive war against a country that did pose a danger to world peace.

Though the doctrine of preventive war is easily abused—as it was in Iraq—sometimes it is a necessary evil. The failure of Britain and France to wage a preventive war against Nazi Germany in the mid-1930s cost the world millions of lives. Will the same be said someday about the failure to prevent Iran from developing nuclear weapons?

≈

PART II.
PRESIDENT OBAMA'S FIRST-
TERM APPROACH TO IRAN

I SUPPORTED PRESIDENT OBAMA when *he first ran for president, though I had originally supported Hillary Clinton during the primaries. I supported Senator Obama over Senator McCain even though I had serious doubts about some of his foreign policy positions, especially with regard to Iran, because I believed both candidates would support Israel, as they promised during the campaign. On domestic issues—health care, a woman's right to choose, criminal justice, and others—I was enthusiastically in favor of Obama, because I have always been a liberal democrat. Here is how I explained the reasons I supported Obama over McCain:*

> I am a strong supporter of Israel (though sometimes critical of specific policies). I am also a strong supporter of Barack Obama (though I favored Hillary Clinton during the primaries). I am now getting dozens of e-mails asking me how as a supporter of Israel I can vote for Barack Obama. Let me explain.
>
> I think that on the important issues relating to Israel, both Senator McCain and Senator Obama score very high. During the debates each candidate has gone out of his and her way to emphasize strong support for Israel as an American ally and a bastion of democracy in a dangerous neighborhood. They have also expressed support for Israel's right to defend itself against the nuclear threat posed

by Iran, which has sworn to wipe Israel off the map, and the need to prevent another Holocaust.

There may be some difference in nuance among the candidates, especially with regard to negotiations with Iran, but supporters of Israel should not base their voting decision on which party or which candidates support Israel more enthusiastically. In the United States, Israel is not a divisive issue, and voting for president is not a referendum on support for Israel, at least among the major parties.

I want to keep it that way. I want to make sure that support for Israel remains strong both among liberals and conservatives. It is clear that extremists on both sides of the political spectrum hate Israel, because they hate liberal democracies, because they tend to have a special place in their heart for tyrannical regimes, and because they often have strange views with regard to anything Jewish. The extreme left, as represented by Noam Chomsky, Ralph Nader, Cynthia McKinney, Norman Finkelstein, and, most recently, Jimmy Carter has little good to say about the Jewish state. But nor does the extreme right, as represented by Pat Buchanan, Robert Novak, Joseph Sobran, and David Duke. When it comes to Israel there is little difference between the extreme right and the extreme left. Nor is there much of a difference between the centrist political left and the centrist political right: both generally support Israel. Among Israel's strongest supporters have always been Ted Kennedy, Harry Reid, Nancy Pelosi, Barney Frank, Hillary Clinton, and Barack Obama. The same is true of the centrist political right, as represented by Mitt Romney, George W. Bush, Orrin Hatch, and John McCain.

Why then do I favor Obama over McCain? First, because I support him on policies unrelated to Israel, such as the Supreme Court, women's rights, separation of church and state, and the economy. But I also prefer Obama to McCain on the issue of Israel. How can I say that if I have just acknowledged that on the issues they both seem to support Israel to an equal degree? The reason is because I think it is better for Israel to have a liberal supporter in the White House than to have a conservative supporter in the Oval Office. Obama's views on Israel will have greater impact on young people, on Europe, on the media, and on others who tend to identify with the liberal perspective. Although I believe that centrist liberals in general tend to support Israel, I acknowledge that support from the left seems to be weakening as support from the right strengthens. The election of Barack Obama—a liberal supporter of Israel—may enhance Israel's position among wavering liberals.

As I travel around university campuses both in the United States and abroad, I see radical academics trying to present Israel as the darling of the right and anathema to the left. As a liberal supporter of Israel, I try to combat that false image. Nothing could help more in this important effort to shore up liberal support for Israel than the election of a liberal president who strongly supports Israel and who is admired by liberals throughout the world. That is among the important reasons why I support Barack Obama for president.[71]

Following Obama's election, I became more concerned about his Iran policy and I stepped up my criticism, as the following articles, written during his first term, will demonstrate.

A. *Linking Iran to Palestinian Statehood: A Mistake*[72]

> The task of forming an international coalition to
> thwart Iran's nuclear program will be made easier
> if progress is made in peace negotiations between
> Israel and the Palestinians, White House Chief of
> Staff Rahm Emanuel has said, according to sources
> in Washington. Israeli TV stations had reported
> Monday night that Emanuel had actually linked
> the two matters, saying that the efforts to stop
> Iran hinged on peace talks with the Palestinians.
> —*Jerusalem Post*, 4 May 2009

Rahm Emanuel is a good man and a good friend of Israel, but in
a highly publicized recent statement he linked American efforts
to stop Iran from developing nuclear weapons to Israeli efforts
toward establishing a Palestinian state. This is dangerous.

I have long favored the two-state solution, as do most Israelis
and American supporters of Israel. I have also long opposed
civilian settlements deep into the West Bank. I hope that Israel
does make efforts, as it has in the past, to establish a Palestinian
state as part of an overall peace between the Jewish state and its
Arab and Muslim neighbors.

Israel in 2000–2001 offered the Palestinians a state in the
entire Gaza Strip and more than 95 percent of the West Bank,
with its capital in Jerusalem and a $35 billion compensation
package for the refugees. Yassir Arafat rejected the offer and
instead began the second intifada, in which nearly 5,000 people
were killed. I hope that Israel once again offers the Palestinians

a contiguous, economically viable, politically independent state in exchange for a real peace, with security, without terrorism, and without any claim to "return" four million alleged refugees as a way of destroying Israel by demography rather than violence.

But the threat from a nuclear Iran is existential and immediate for Israel. It also poses dangers to the entire region, as well as to the US—not only from the possibility that a nation directed by suicidal leaders would order a nuclear attack on Israel or its allies, but from the likelihood that nuclear material could end up in the hands of Hezbollah, Hamas, or even Al Qaeda.

Israel has the right, indeed the obligation, to take this threat seriously and to consider it as a first priority. It will be far easier for Israel to make peace with the Palestinians if it does not have to worry about the threat of a nuclear attack or a dirty bomb. It will also be easier for Israel to end its occupation of the West Bank if Iran is not arming and inciting Hamas, Hezbollah, and other enemies of Israel to terrorize Israel with rockets and suicide bombers.

In this respect, Emanuel has it exactly backward: if there is any linkage, it goes the other way—defanging Iran will promote the end of the occupation and the two-state solution. Threatening not to help Israel in relation to Iran unless it moves toward a two-state solution first is likely to backfire.

After all, Israel is a democracy, and in the end the people decide. A recent poll published in *Haaretz* concluded that 66 percent of Israelis favored a preemptive military strike against Iran's nuclear facilities, with 75 percent of those saying they would still favor such a strike even if the US were opposed.

Israel's new government will accept a two-state solution if they are persuaded that it will really be a solution—that it will assure peace and an end to terrorist and nuclear threats to Israeli citizens. I have known Prime Minister Netanyahu for thirty-five years, and I recently had occasion to spend some time with Foreign Minister Avigdor Lieberman. I am convinced that despite their occasional tough talk, both want to see an end to this conflict.

Israelis have been scarred by what happened in Gaza. Israel ended the occupation, removed all of the settlers, and left behind millions of dollars' worth of agricultural and other facilities designed to make the Gaza into an economically viable democracy. Land for peace is what they sought. Instead they got land for rocket attacks against their children, their women, and their elderly. No one wants to see a repeat of this trade-off.

Emanuel's statements were viewed with alarm in Israel because most Israelis, though they want to like President Obama, are nervous about his policies toward Israel. They are prepared to accept pressure regarding the settlements, but they worry that the Obama administration may be ready to compromise, or at least threaten to compromise, Israel's security if its newly elected government does not submit to pressure on the settlements.

Making peace with the Palestinians will be extremely complicated. It will take time. It may or may not succeed in the end, depending on whether the Palestinians will continue to want their own state less than they want to see the end of the Jewish state. Israel should not be held hostage to the Iranian nuclear threat by the difficulty of making peace with the Palestinians. Israel may be rebuffed again, especially if Palestinian radicals believe that such a rebuff will soften American action against Iran. In the meantime, Iran will continue in its efforts to develop nuclear weapons.

That cannot be allowed to happen, regardless of progress on the ground toward peace with the Palestinians. These two issues must be delinked if either is to succeed. There are other ways of encouraging Israel to make peace with the Palestinians. Nuclear blackmail is not one of them.

B. *Obama's Legacy and the Iranian Bomb: Neville Chamberlain was remembered for appeasing Germany, not his progressive social programs.*[73]

The gravest threat faced by the world today is a nuclear armed Iran. Of all the nations capable of producing nuclear weapons, Iran is the only one that might use them to attack an enemy.

There are several ways in which Iran could use nuclear weapons. The first is by dropping an atomic bomb on Israel, as its leaders have repeatedly threatened to do.

The second way in which Iran could use nuclear weapons would be to hand them off to its surrogates, Hezbollah or Hamas. A third way would be for a terrorist group, such as Al Qaeda, to get its hands on Iranian nuclear material. It could do so with the consent of Iran or by working with rogue elements within the Iranian regime.

Finally, Iran could use its nuclear weapons without ever detonating a bomb. By constantly threatening Israel with nuclear annihilation, it could engender so much fear among Israelis as to incite mass immigration, a brain drain, or a significant decline in people moving to Israel.

These are the specific ways in which Iran could use nuclear weapons, primarily against the Jewish state. But there are other ways in which a nuclear armed Iran would endanger the world.

First, it would cause an arms race in which every nation in the Middle East would seek to obtain nuclear weapons.

Second, it would almost certainly provoke Israel into engaging in either a preemptive or retaliatory attack, thus inflaming the entire region or inciting further attacks against Israel by Hezbollah and Hamas.

Third, it would provide Iran with a nuclear umbrella under which it could accelerate its efforts at regional hegemony. Had Iraq operated under a nuclear umbrella when it invaded Kuwait in 1990, Saddam Hussein's forces would still be in Kuwait.

Fourth, it would embolden the most radical elements in the Middle East to continue their war of words and deeds against the United States and its allies.

And finally, it would inevitably unleash the law of unintended consequences: simply put, nobody knows the extent of the harm a nuclear armed Iran could produce.

In these respects, allowing Iran to obtain nuclear weapons is somewhat analogous to the decision by the victors of World War I to allow Nazi Germany to rearm during the 1930s. Even the Nazis were surprised at this complacency. Joseph Goebbels expected the French and British to prevent the Nazis from rebuilding Germany's war machine.

In 1940, Goebbels told a group of German journalists that if he had been the French premier when Hitler came to power, he would have said, "The new Reich chancellor is the man who wrote *Mein Kampf*, which says this and that. This man cannot be tolerated in our vicinity. Either he disappears or we march!"

But, Goebbels continued, "They didn't do it. They left us alone and let us slip through the risky zone, and we were able to sail around all dangerous reefs. And when we were done, and well armed, better than they, then they started the war!"

Most people today are not aware that British Prime Minister Neville Chamberlain helped restore Great Britain's financial stability during the Great Depression and also passed legislation to extend unemployment benefits, pay pensions to retired workers, and otherwise help those hit hard by the slumping economy. But history does remember his failure to confront Hitler. That is Chamberlain's enduring legacy.

So too will Iran's construction of nuclear weapons, if it manages to do so in the next few years, become President Barack Obama's enduring legacy. Regardless of his passage of health care reform and regardless of whether he restores jobs and helps the economy recover, Mr. Obama will be remembered for allowing Iran to obtain nuclear weapons. History will not treat kindly any leader who allows so much power to be accumulated by the world's first suicide nation—a nation whose leaders have not only expressed but, during the Iran-Iraq war, demonstrated a willingness to sacrifice millions of their own people to an apocalyptic mission of destruction.

If Iran were to become a nuclear power, there would be plenty of blame to go around. Chamberlain, too, was not entirely to blame for Hitler's initial triumphs. He became prime minister after his predecessors allowed Germany to rearm. Nevertheless, it is Chamberlain who has come to symbolize the failure to prevent Hitler's ascendancy. So too will Mr. Obama come to symbolize the failure of the West if Iran acquires nuclear weapons on his watch.

c. *The Obama Administration's Conflicting Messages on Iran*[74]

The Obama administration is sending conflicting and confusing messages both to Iran and to those who fear an Iranian nuclear weapon. According to the *New York Times*, defense secretary Robert M. Gates sent a top secret memorandum to White House officials bemoaning the fact that the United States simply has no policy in place to prevent Iran from developing nuclear weapons.[75] At the same time, it is telling Israel that although Iran has threatened to wipe it off the map, the Jewish state should not take military action to prevent a second Holocaust. Indeed former national security adviser Zbigniew Brzezinski, who has participated in White House discussions concerning the Middle East, has threatened that if Israel tries to destroy Iran's nuclear weapon facilities, the United States is fully capable of shooting Israeli jets out of the air.

Although Gates subsequently denied that his memo, which he acknowledges writing, was intended as a "wake-up call," a senior White House official has confirmed that it was just that. There is no evidence, however, that the White House is prepared to confront the grave threat posed by a nuclear Iran. The policy that seems to be emerging from the White House is one called "containment." But what is containment? It is little more than an acknowledgment of failure. Containment implies that the United States will not succeed in preventing Iran from securing nuclear weapons, but rather it will accept such an eventuality and seek to deter the use of nuclear weapons by threats and by the deployment of defensive measures. The analogy that proponents of containment point to is North Korea, which has nuclear weapons but has thus far been "contained" from using them. But there are vast differences between North Korea and Iran.

North Korea is a secular Communist regime that is risk averse and that has no sworn existential enemies. The goal of its leaders is simply to remain in power and maintain their totalitarian control over their people. Iran is a theocratic, apocalyptic regime that believes that it has a religious obligation to destroy Israel and threaten the United States. Iran, unlike North Korea, also operates through surrogates, such as Hezbollah, Hamas, and other smaller terrorist groups. They could hand off nuclear material to such groups, or to sympathetic individuals, for use as dirty bombs directed against its enemies.

When he ran for president, Barack Obama pledged not to allow Iran to develop nuclear weapons. He claimed to understand that a nuclear Iran would be a game changer and a direct threat to the United States and its allies. He now seems to be softening his position and that of the United States government.

If in fact the United States is prepared to accept a nuclear Iran, then it has no right to require Israel to accept the risks posed by a nuclear armed country that has overtly threatened its destruction. Every country in the world has the inherent right to protect its citizens from a nuclear attack. Israel, a nation that Obama has himself acknowledged was built on the ashes of one Holocaust, certainly has the right to take military action to prevent a second

Holocaust, especially at the hands of a country that has explicitly threatened to wipe it off the map.

The world ignored the explicit threats of one tyrant who threatened to destroy the Jewish people in the 1930s, and he nearly succeeded in the 1940s. Israel cannot be expected to ignore Hitler's successor, who while denying the first Holocaust, threatens a second one.

The United States has promised to regard a nuclear attack on Israel as a nuclear attack on its own country, but Iran does not credit such threats, since it appears that the Obama administration has already broken its promise not to accept a nuclear Iran. Elie Wiesel put it well when he said that the Holocaust has taught the Jewish people to "believe the threats of our enemies more than the promises of our friends." Iran's promise to destroy Israel must be taken seriously, not only by Israel but by the United States. If the United States is not prepared to stop Iran from acquiring the nuclear weapons necessary to wipe Israel off the map, then Israel must be prepared to protect itself.

I am not suggesting that Israel *should* attack Iran's nuclear weapons facilities. I don't know enough about the military considerations that should go into such an existential decision. But I am asserting, in unqualified terms, that Israel has an absolute *right*—legally, morally, politically—to take such an action if it deems it necessary to protect its citizens from a threatened nuclear attack. This is especially the case if Secretary Gates was correct when he wrote in his memorandum that the United States "lacks a policy to thwart Iran," as the *New York Times* headline announced. Someone must thwart Iran. An Iran with nuclear weapons simply poses too great a threat to the world to be accepted—or "contained."

D. *There Will Never Be Peace if Iran Gets the Bomb*[76]

Now that the WikiLeaks reveal widespread Arab support for the military option against Iran's nuclear facilities to be put on the table,[77] the time has come to reassess United States policy toward the Ahmadinejad regime.

Even if Israel freezes settlement building, the Palestinians come to the negotiating table, and an agreement is reached about borders, refugees, and Jerusalem, there will still be no real peace in the Middle East—if Iran continues on its determined path toward developing deliverable nuclear weapons. Despite noble efforts by the United States to bring Israel and the Palestinians to the peace process, the inability to achieve a real peace will be largely the fault of the deeply flawed American policy toward Iran.

The policy of the United States seems to be that a nuclear Iran is inevitable, that sanctions may delay but not prevent the Iranians from developing the bomb, and that a policy of containment is the best we can hope for. But containment is not a policy; it is an admission of failure. A nuclear Iran cannot be contained, because it operates largely through surrogates such as Hezbollah, Hamas, and other terrorist groups. It can direct these surrogates to take actions that do not leave Iranian fingerprints. Currently these actions are limited to Hezbollah aiming rockets at Israel's heartland and Hamas firing improvised rockets at Israeli civilians. If these groups—which oppose any peace with Israel—could operate under the protection of an Iranian nuclear umbrella, they would constantly provoke retaliatory and preventive military actions. These actions might well force the Palestinian Authority to violate agreements they made with Israel. Moreover, an Israeli population constantly under the threat of a nuclear Holocaust from a nation whose leader has called for Israel to be wiped off the map may demand that preventive military action be taken. Any such action by Israel would provoke an immediate response from Hezbollah and Hamas, if not from the Palestinian Authority.

Nor would a nuclear Iran limit its mischief to Israel. Now that it has obtained medium-range ballistic missiles from North Korea, it might feel adventurous enough to export nuclear terrorism to other parts of the Middle East, North Africa, and Europe. President Barack Obama understated the threat when he said that a nuclear Iran would be "a game changer." It would be unmitigated disaster, threatening world peace, putting an end to any hope of nuclear nonproliferation, and engendering the greatest arms race in modern history.

The fault for this disaster would be equally shared by the Bush and the Obama administrations. Under George Bush's watch, the United States issued its notorious National Security Estimate of November 2007, which essentially denied that Iran was seeking to develop nuclear weapons.[78] This report was known to be false at the time it was issued since American intelligence became aware of the nuclear weapons facility at Qom before the report was issued. The publication of this report sent a powerful message to Iran: the Americans have fallen for your bait-and-switch game in which you hide your capacity to develop nuclear weapons under the cover of purported civilian use. This has encouraged the Iranians to move full-throttle ahead on their program. At the same time, the Bush administration changed Israel's green light to yellow and then to red as it related to United States approval of an Israeli strike against Iran's nuclear facilities. The end result was that Iran felt no real constraints on continuing to develop its nuclear weapons capacity in a pretextual civilian context.

The Obama administration appears to have taken any military option off the table, relying instead on its enhanced package of sanctions. Secretary of Defense Gates has been explicit about this and the Iranians have been listening. It makes absolutely no sense to take the military option off the table, even—perhaps especially—if one is reluctant to deploy it. As George Washington taught us in his first address to Congress: "To be prepared for war is one of the most effectual means of preserving peace." Israel's prime minister echoed President Washington when he recently said, "The simple paradox is this: if the international community, led by the United States, hopes to stop Iran's nuclear program without resorting to military action, it will have to convince Iran that it is prepared to take such action." What is it that American policymakers don't seem to understand about this self-evident proposition?

The man most responsible for both the Bush and Obama administration's failure with regard to Iran is Secretary of Defense Robert Gates, whose tenure has straddled both the issuance of the false National Security Estimate and the decision to take the military option off the table. He is Iran's favorite American facilitator. Although he soon plans to leave office, there are no signs—certainly none visible to Iran—that his failed policies with regard to Iran's nuclear program will end with his too-long tenure.

The biblical prophet cautioned "peace, peace, and there is no peace." This tragic prophecy will become a sad reality if Israel and the Palestinian Authority make great sacrifices in an effort to bring peace to their people, only to see that peace shattered by a shortsighted American policy that allows Iran to hold a nuclear sword of Damocles over the entire region.

E. *Why I Worry about Obama's Policy Toward Israel's Security*[79]

The line in the sand, for me, has always been Israel's security. I decided to vote for Barack Obama, having previously favored Hillary Clinton, only after Obama went to Sderot and affirmed Israel's right to do whatever was necessary to stop rockets from targeting Israeli civilians. When Obama became president, I was not surprised that he took a tough stance against Israeli settlements on the West Bank, which I too have opposed since 1973. I noted with satisfaction that although Obama criticized the settlements on the West Bank, he did not criticize the security barrier that was built, in part, on land captured in the 1967 war. I also noted with satisfaction that the Obama administration categorically rejected the Goldstone Report—a report that was entirely inconsistent with candidate Obama's statements at Sderot.

I began to get worried about the Obama administration when Rahm Emanuel appeared to link American support for Israel's security with Israeli actions regarding the settlements. I became even more concerned when Vice President Biden and General David Petraeus were quoted as suggesting that Israel's actions could affect American casualties in Iraq and Afghanistan. Although Emanuel, Biden, and Petraeus quickly distanced themselves from this linkage argument, it continues to have a life of its own, despite its falsity, as evidenced by the fact that while Israel was seeking to make peace in 2000–2001 by creating a Palestinian state on the West Bank and in Gaza with a capital in East Jerusalem, Al Qaeda was planning the 9/11 attack. So Israel's "good" actions did nothing to make America safe from Islamic terrorism. On the other hand, when Israel took tough action against Gaza last year in Operation Cast Lead, Israel's "bad" actions did not increase American casualties in Iraq and Afghanistan. It is also dangerous because its implication is that Israel must cease to exist: the basic complaint that Muslim extremists have against Israel is not what the Jewish state does, but what it is: a secular, non-Muslim, democracy that promotes equal rights for women, gays, Christians, and others. Regardless of what Israel does or doesn't do, its very existence will be anathema to Muslim extremists. The only action Israel could take to mollify such extremists would be to commit politicide.

Another source of concern for me has been the Obama policy regarding Iran. Secretary William Gates wrote a memo in which he acknowledged that America has no real policy that is likely to prevent Iran from securing nuclear weapons.[80] Instead the Obama administration is moving toward a policy of "containment," which is no policy at all, but rather is an implicit admission of failure. At the same time that it has been weak toward Iran, it has been firm toward Israel in telling an ally that has been threatened with nuclear destruction that it may not exercise its inherent right to prevent its citizens from becoming victims of a second Holocaust advocated by a tyrant who denies that the first occurred.

So I am worried about the direction the Obama administration seems to be taking with regard to Israel's security. I will not join the chorus of condemnation by right wingers directed against the Obama policy with regard to the settlements, or even with regard to a divided Jerusalem. The Obama administration has not yet crossed my line in the sand. I hope it never does so, but if it does, I will be extremely critical. In the meantime, those of us who supported Obama must continue to press him against compromising Israel's security and against suggesting a false and dangerous linkage between Israel's actions and the safety of American troops.

F.   *The Disclosure of Arab Views on Iran's Nuclear*
     Plans Has Made a Military Strike More Likely[81]

Former US secretary of state Henry Stimson famously declared that "gentlemen do not read each other's mail," referring to Japanese diplomatic cables the US had uncovered by breaking Japan's military code. Today, everybody reads everybody else's diplomatic mail if they can get their hands on it.

Mostly, this is a bad thing because secrecy—when properly used—can serve the interest of peace and security. Nations have the right to keep secrets from other nations, although they generally overdo it. But individuals do not have the right to decide for themselves when to reveal state secrets. The soldier who broke into governmental computers committed a serious crime and will be punished for it. The question is whether those who released the secrets to the press, namely WikiLeaks, are complicit in the crime.

The newspapers that published leaked material make a compelling case for the decision to select certain items for publication while withholding others. The press is, after all, part of our informal system of checks and balances.

But Secretary of State Hillary Clinton is surely correct when she warns that WikiLeaks poses a danger not only to the US but to international diplomacy, while at the same time trying to minimize the actual harm done by these particular disclosures.

The disclosure that virtually every Arab country, including Egypt and Saudi Arabia, would favor a military attack, as a last resort, to prevent Iran from developing nuclear weapons could have a discernible effect on the policies of several countries. Israel, of course, has long insisted that the military option be kept on the table. The disclosure that North Korea has delivered missiles to Iran may well frighten European countries into considering the option of military action if sanctions don't work.

There is additional information, not revealed by WikiLeaks, suggesting that although sanctions are having some effect on Iran's economy, Tehran has decided to move forward with its nuclear weapons program. Computer bugs and the assassination of nuclear scientists may be slowing the process but are not likely to stop it.

The leaks confirm the US has made two disastrous decisions in dealing with Iran. The first came in 2007, when it released a misleading National Intelligence Estimate conveying the impression Iran had stopped its nuclear weapons program.[82] The second was the more recent statements by Secretary of Defense Robert Gates that appear to have taken any military option off the table. These mistakes have encouraged Iran to move ahead with its program.

A third mistake is to believe that there can be real peace in the Middle East with an Iranian nuclear sword of Damocles hanging over the head of Israel. Even if Israel were to continue the settlement freeze and negotiate borders with the Palestinian Authority, the Iranians could ruin any prospect of permanent peace by unleashing Hezbollah and Hamas—which oppose any peace with Israel—to target Israeli civilians.

President Obama understated the threat when he said a nuclear Iran would be "a game changer." It would be a disaster, threatening Middle East peace, putting an end to any hope of nuclear nonproliferation, and engendering the greatest arms race in modern history.

Now that it has been made public that Arab nations favor a military attack, it will become more difficult for these countries to condemn Israel if it was to decide on a surgical strike. This public disclosure might embolden Israel to consider such a strike as a last resort.

So the leaking of secret information may have grave, even if unintended, consequences. We need new laws and new technologies to cope with the apparent ease with which low-level functionaries can access and download the most secret of information. But there will always be those willing to break the law and suffer the consequences for what they believe is a higher purpose; and it is always just a matter of time until the techno-thieves catch up to the techno-cops. We will have to learn to live with the reality that there is no absolute assurance that "gentlemen" (and others) will not be reading each other's mail.

Israel and the US: Behind the Tension—
Is Friendship a One-Way Street?[83]

One important lesson to be learned from the turmoil in the Middle East is that there is only one democracy that the United States can always count on to remain a strong ally. That democracy is Israel. No one knows whether any or all of the Arab states that are currently in flux will pull an "Iran" on us—turning from friend to foe in the blink of an Ayatollah.

Even if some of the blame for this uncertainty falls on us for supporting friendly dictators, from the shah to Hosni Mubarak to King Abdullah, the reality is that the United States simply cannot count on the increasingly vocal Arab street to support American interests. That is precisely why we have, rightly or wrongly, felt the need to cozy up to Arab tyrants who promise us stability in exchange for financial and military support.

Not so with Israel. But here's the pressing outstanding question: Does the United States reciprocate, or are we a fair-weather friend to our stalwart ally?

So far, we've been principled enough to reciprocate. United States administrations may prefer some Israeli electoral outcomes to others. We may prefer certain Israeli leaders over others. But in the end, we must recognize that Israel is a stable democracy that does not need propping up from the outside.

The military aid we give Israel is not designed to protect a regime against its own citizens, as it is with regard to the aid to Jordan and Egypt. The purpose of our assistance to Israel is to protect it from external enemies like Iran, sworn to its destruction.

The people of Israel may not love a particular American president or administration, but they love America and what we stand for. And Israel helps America—with intelligence gathering, development of military weapons, cyber technology defense, and in numerous other ways. The relationship is a model of symbiosis.

But recent events in the Middle East, particularly the haste with which we abandoned Mubarak, our most loyal Arab ally, have raised questions among some Israelis as to whether Israel can always count on the United States.

Skeptical Israelis wonder how this, or any other, American administration would react to a demand from the Arab street across the entire Middle East or the United States to abandon Israel. They recall how quickly we abandoned the shah and how responsive our government has been to the demands of protesters in Tunisia and elsewhere.

While recognizing the enormous difference between democratic Israel and the tyrannical regimes against which the Arab street is now rising, these concerned Israelis are contemplating a worst-case scenario. They fear that history has shown that a friend in desperate need is a friend often betrayed.

This skepticism is not necessarily fueled by any criticism of the United States, but rather by a realistic recognition that America has its own national interests, which it will always place over the interests of even its staunchest allies. The United States is, for better or worse, the world's most important superpower, and it must necessarily serve as a kind of policeman to the entire world.

I'm not alone in believing that it will always be in America's interests to support Israel because of its commitment to values akin to our own. But there are other Americans—from those on the extreme right like Senator Rand Paul, to so-called realists like Stephen Walt and John Mearsheimer, to those on the extreme left like Noam Chomsky—who would see no problem in abandoning Israel at the drop of a keffiyeh.

Accordingly, though most Israelis believe that America will always support its survival, many refuse to count on it. That's why they developed a long-term strategy of self-reliance. The attitude of many Israelis can perhaps best be summed up by the important lesson Elie Wiesel has taught all Jews to learn from the Holocaust: "Always believe the threat of your enemies more than the promises of your friends."

Iran's recent attempt to ship arms to Hamas[85] in Gaza is an act of
war committed by the Iranian government against the Israeli government. The Israeli navy seized the ship, loaded with weapons
designed to kill Israeli civilians, and traced the weapons back to
Iran. Nor is this the first act of war that would justify a military
response by Israel under international law. Iran has sent other
boatloads of antipersonnel weapons to Hamas and Hezbollah.
In addition, back in 1992, the Iranian leaders planned and authorized a deadly attack on Israel's embassy in Argentina. That
bombing, which was carried out by Iranian agents, constituted
a direct armed attack on the state of Israel, since its embassy is
part of its sovereign territory. Moreover, the Iranian government
has publicly declared war on Israel by calling for it "to be wiped
off the map."

Under international law, these acts of war—known as casus
belli—fully justify an Israeli armed response. Even the UN
Charter authorizes a unilateral response to an armed attack.
Providing weapons to a declared enemy in the face of an
embargo has historically been deemed an armed attack under
the law of war, especially when those providing the weapons

intend for them to be used against the enemy's civilians. So too is the bombing of an embassy.

Two other recent events enhance Israel's right use military means to prevent Iran from continuing to arm Israel's enemies. The recent disaster in Japan has shown the world the extraordinary dangers posed by nuclear radiation. If anybody ever doubted the power of a dirty bomb to devastate a nation, both physically and psychologically, those doubts have been eliminated by what is now going on in Japan. If Iran were to develop nuclear weapons, the next ship destined to Gaza might contain a nuclear dirty bomb and Israel might not intercept that one. A dirty bomb detonated in tiny Israel would cause incalculable damage to civilian life.

Moreover, the recent killings in Itamar[86] of a family including three children demonstrate how weapons are used by Israel's enemies against civilians in violation of the laws of war. Even babies are targeted by those armed by Iran. Hamas praised the murders.

Israel has the right to prevent its civilians from being murdered by Iranian weapons, especially weapons of mass destruction. Iran would have no legal standing to protest a surgical attack on its nuclear facilities that are designing weapons that could be used to achieve Iran's declared goal of wiping Israel off the map and killing millions of its citizens. The leaders of Iran have publicly declared that a nuclear exchange, killing millions of Jews and Muslims, would be acceptable to them because it would destroy Israel while only damaging Islam. A suicide nation cannot be deterred by the threat of retaliation. Israel's only realistic option may be a preventive military strike of the kind it conducted against Iraq's nuclear reactor in 1981. That surgical attack may have saved countless lives at the cost of one single casualty. By the way, Iran too tried to destroy Iraq's nuclear reactor, but failed. Certainly Israel has the right to do what Iran itself tried to do—namely prevent a lethal enemy from developing weapons capable of mass murder of its citizens.

This is not to say that Israel should attack Iran's nuclear reactors now. That it has the right to do so does not mean that it should not wait for a more opportune time. The law of war does not require an immediate military response to an armed attack. The nation attacked can postpone its counterattack without waiving its right. The military option should always be a last resort after all other efforts have failed. It may well be that efforts to permanently disable Iran's nuclear computers will succeed. Although it is unlikely that economic sanctions will ever persuade Iran's ideological zealots to end their nuclear weapons program, a combination of quasi-military, tough economic and diplomatic sanctions may slow it down to a point where the military option can be postponed. But under no circumstances should the military option ever be taken off the table. Israel must preserve its ability to exercise its fundamental right of preventive self-defense. If possible, it should act together with other allies. But if necessary, it has the right to act alone to protect its citizens. Nearly everybody hopes that it won't come to that, but hope is not a policy. As George Washington cautioned in his second inaugural address, "To be prepared for war is one of the most effectual means of preserving peace."

1. *WikiLeaks Contradicts Obama Administration on Iran*[87]

The recent disclosure by WikiLeaks* proves that the Obama administration, and its water carrier, J Street, were dead wrong in repeatedly asserting that the only way to get Arab support for tough policies toward Iran's nuclear weapons program is for Israel to end the occupation of the West Bank. There are good reasons for Israel to reach an agreement with the Palestinians leading to a two-state solution, but garnering Arab support against Iran is not one of them. The WikiLeaks proved beyond any doubt that Israel's Arab neighbors have a strong, independent basis for wanting to stop Iran from becoming a nuclear weapons power.

The recently released cables establish that Saudi Arabia was pushing the United States to bomb Iranian nuclear sites; these cables never mentioned the Israeli Palestinian conflict. Nor were the Saudis alone in calling for the United States to cut off the "head of the snake." Other Arab nations were banging the drum for a military attack as well. Indeed there is evidence that the

* On 22 November 2010, WikiLeaks began to release a huge number of diplomatic cables including correspondence between the US State Department and the foreign ministries of several Middle Eastern countries.

Saudis and Israelis—who have no diplomatic relations—have discussed military options against their common enemy.[88]

Ever since the Obama administration tried to put pressure on Israel by linking the end of the occupation to Iran, I have pointed out the absurdity of this linkage. But General David Petraeus, Secretary of State Robert Gates, and Vice President Joe Biden have all insisted that the continuing occupation has made Arab states less willing to cooperate with the United States in preventing Iran from developing nuclear bombs. This party line view has been parroted, as usual, by various representatives of J Street.

Not only has this linkage never been true, but we now know that the Obama administration has long been aware that the Arab states are as anxious as Israel about Iran's nuclear ambitions. This information was contained in diplomatic cables that date back months, if not years. Why then would the Obama administration deliberately mislead the public in regard so important a matter? The same question must be asked of the Bush administration, which also misled the public when it came to Iran by releasing the National Security Estimate in November 2007 that falsely concluded that Iran had abandoned its nuclear weapons program.

The answer may well be that both the Obama and Bush administrations realize that nothing short of a military attack will stop Iran from developing deliverable nuclear weapons. Since both administrations have apparently taken any military option off the table, they seem to have accepted a policy of "containment." But containment is not a policy. It is an admission of failure. And failure requires a scapegoat. If Israel does not end the occupation, and Iran does develop nuclear weapons, it will be easy to blame Israel rather than the United States for this game-changing development.

In an op-ed in this past Sunday's *New York Times*,[89] Chas Freeman—the anti-Israel zealot whose nomination to become chair of the National Intelligence Council was withdrawn under pressure—has already tried to cast blame on Israel. He argues that notwithstanding the clear language of the recently released cables, the Gulf Arabs do not want the United States to attack Iran. Nor did the cables, according to Freeman, "demonstrate a basis for Arab-Israeli solidarity against Tehran." This is patent nonsense, reflecting Freeman's bias, rather than reality. He also argues, with typical contempt of history, that the only country that ever says no in the Middle East is Israel, forgetting that Israel has on several occasions offered to end the occupation and accept a two-state solution. Freeman conveniently forgets that when the occupation first began, Israel offered to return the land captured in a defensive war in exchange for peace with its Arab neighbors. All the Arab states convened in Khartoum and issued their three famous *nos*: no negotiation, no recognition, no peace. So much for Freeman's credibility.

The truth is that the Palestinians have marginalized themselves in the Middle East by rejecting offers that the Arab states have urged them to accept. Iran is the 800-pound gorilla in the area, and all the other countries in the Middle East recognize that and have a common interest in preventing so irresponsible a regime from working together with North Korea to develop nuclear rockets.

The WikiLeaks prove what many of us have been saying for years: that the United States, as the leader of the free world, must stop Iran from developing nuclear weapons—whatever it takes. Although an air and rocket attack should remain an absolutely last resort, this military option must remain on the table. If all else fails and the United States must resort to military action, the Arab world will support such action (at least in private), regardless of whether Israel and the Palestinian Authority finally make peace.

Now that Prime Minister Benjamin Netanyahu is back in Israel and President Obama is traveling around Europe, it is time to assess the effect their dueling speeches have had on the prospects for peace.

There is one factual conclusion on which the Israelis and the Palestinians completely agree: following President Obama's recent speech[91]—and repeated explanation of it—on the Israel-Palestine conflict, we are further than ever from peace negotiations. Obama has managed, in one fell swoop, to harden the positions of both sides and to create distrust of him by Israelis and Palestinians alike.

My criticism of the president is not directed at whether he is pro-Israel or anti-Israel, pro-Palestinian or anti-Palestinian. In fact, I believe that his actions have not been motivated by any antagonism toward the Jewish state. He simply does not understand the dynamics of Middle East negotiation. I am disappointed in him not because I support Israel (which I do), but because I support peace based on a two-state solution. I agree with Obama about his ends while disagreeing about his means.

Indeed there is little in the content of the president's statements with which I disagree. Rather, it is with his negotiating strategy, his constant need to explain himself, and his utter tone deafness to the music, as distinguished from the lyrics.

The president has asked the Israelis to agree to negotiate new borders based on the 1967 lines, with land swaps. But he did so without asking the Palestinians to agree to drop their demand that millions of so-called "refugees"—those who fled or left Israel during the 1947–49 Arab attacks against the Jewish state, and their descendants—be allowed to "return" to Israel. New borders would be meaningless if this demographic bomb were to be dropped on Israel, turning it into yet another Arab state with a Palestinian majority.

Everyone knows, as a matter of reality, that this is not going to happen, just as everyone knows that Israel will eventually give up most of the West Bank as it did the Gaza Strip. But it is critical to any successful negotiation that these two issues— borders and "the right to return"—be negotiated together. The Israelis will never agree to generous borders for the Palestinians unless they are assured that their identity as the nation-state of the Jewish people will not be demographically undercut by "the right of return." And the Palestinians will never give up their emotionally charged right of return unless that is an unambiguous prerequisite to achieving statehood with generous borders. The Obama strategy—to demand generous borders from Israel first and leave the right of return to subsequent negotiations—is a prescription for stalemate.

The president also helped cement the status quo by expressing his agreement with Israel's refusal to negotiate with a Palestinian government that includes Hamas—unless that terrorist group first renounces violence, accepts Israel, and supports prior agreements. The current position of the Israeli government is to invite the Palestinian Authority to begin negotiations now, but to insist, before any final agreement is reached, that Hamas either accept the president's current conditions or be excluded from the government. By going further than the Israeli government—by seeming to justify an Israeli refusal even to begin negotiations with the Palestinian Authority until Hamas accepts those conditions or the Palestinian Authority rejects Hamas—the president has made it harder for the Netanyahu government to resist the demands of Israeli extremists who oppose all negotiations.

Netanyahu originally planned to come to Washington with a generous peace proposal to entice the Palestinians back to the negotiating table. But Obama painted him into a corner and made him change his script by notifying him, as he was about to board his plane, that the president was going to call for Israel to return to its 1949–1967 lines without also calling for the Palestinians to give up their right of return. By thus preempting the prime minister, he forced him to become more defensive of Israel's bargaining positions and less willing to offer specific, generous concessions. The result was a powerful speech in defense of Israel by Netanyahu, an overwhelmingly positive response from Congress, and a movement away from peace negotiations.

All in all, the president's well-intentioned efforts to jump-start the peace process have backfired, not so much because he favors one side over the other, but because of the ham-handedness of his negotiation strategy. A negotiator or mediator whose statements move the parties further away from the negotiating table than they were before he spoke deserves a failing grade in the science of negotiation.

What the president should have done is to insist that both parties immediately agree to sit down and negotiate without any preconditions.

It's not too late. But it will take yet another "explanation" of what President Obama really meant in his ill-advised speech.

K. *Warning Iran Against Hitting "Soft"*
   American Targets[92]

The Iranian government has now made crystal clear that it is at war not only with Israel and Zionism but with Jewish communities throughout the world. As Iran's Rafah news website—identified with President Mahmoud Ahmadinejad—threatened last month, Iran plans to "take the war beyond the borders of Iran, and beyond the borders of the region." And last week an Iranian news agency headline declared that "Israeli people must be annihilated."

These and other recent threats have, according to news reports, led Israeli and American authorities to believe that Iran is preparing attacks against Israeli embassies and consulates worldwide, as well as against Jewish houses of prayer, schools, community centers, restaurants, and other soft targets.

If this were to happen, it would not be the first time that Iranian agents have bombed or attacked Israeli and Jewish targets in distant countries. Back in 1992, Iranian agents blew up the Israeli embassy and a Jewish community center in Buenos Aires, killing and injuring hundreds of civilians, many of whom were children. The Argentine government conducted a thorough criminal investigation and indicted several Iranian officials, but those officials were well beyond the reach of Argentine legal authorities and remain at liberty.

The US government should deem any Iranian attack against Israeli or Jewish soft targets in America to be an armed military attack on the US—to which the US will retaliate militarily at a time and place of its choosing. Washington should not treat such an attack as the Argentine authorities did, merely as a criminal act.

Under international law, an attack on an embassy is an attack both on the embassy's country and on the country in which the embassy is located. And under the charter of the United Nations, an attack against a nation's citizens on its territory is an act of armed aggression that justifies retaliatory military action.

An attack on an American synagogue is no different than an attack on the World Trade Center or on American aviation. We correctly regarded those attacks as acts of war committed by Al Qaeda and facilitated by the government of Afghanistan, and we responded militarily. All American citizens, regardless of their religious affiliation, are equally entitled to the protection of the American military.

US retaliation could take the form of military action against Iran's nuclear facilities. Though such action might be preemptive in its intention, it would be reactive as a matter of international law, since it would be in response to an armed attack by Iran. It wouldn't require Security Council approval, since Article 51 of the UN Charter explicitly preserves the right of member nations to respond to any armed attack.

This is not to argue against such an attack if Iran decides not to go after soft American targets. It may become necessary for our military to target Iranian nuclear facilities if economic sanctions and diplomatic efforts do not succeed and if the Iranian government decides to cross red lines by militarizing its nuclear program and placing it in deep underground bunkers. But the legal justification for such an attack would be somewhat different. It would be predominantly preemptive or preventive, though it would have reactive elements as well, since Iran has armed our enemies in Iraq and caused the death of many American soldiers.

If Israel were compelled to act alone against Iran's nuclear program, it too would be reacting as well as preempting, since Iran has effectively declared war against the Jewish state and its people. Hezbollah leader Hassan Nasrallah recently confirmed Iran's role as Hezbollah's active partner in its war against Israel, claiming that it "could not have been victorious" in its 2006 war without the military support of Tehran. Iran's ongoing support for Hezbollah and Hamas, coupled with its direct participation in the bombing of the Israeli embassy in Buenos Aires, constitute sufficient casus belli to justify a reactive Israeli military strike against the Iranian nuclear program.

The best outcome, of course, would be to deter Iran from both foreign aggression and domestic nuclearization by making the costs too high, even for the most zealous or adventurous Iranian leaders. But for deterrence to succeed where sanctions and other tactics appear to be failing, the threat of military action must be credible. Right now it is not, because Defense Secretary Leon Panetta and other administration officials are sending mixed signals, not only with regard to the US but also with regard to Israel.

The administration must speak with an unambiguous and credible voice that leaves no doubt in the minds of Iranian leaders that America won't tolerate attacks on our citizens or a nuclear armed Iran. As George Washington wisely counseled in his second inaugural address, "To be prepared for war is one of the most effectual means of preserving peace."

≈

PART III.
PRESIDENT OBAMA'S
SECOND-TERM ELECTION
PROMISES REGARDING IRAN

IN JANUARY 2012, I was *in Israel speaking at a conference about Israel's security and economy. I discussed Iran, among other issues. The speaker following me was Prime Minister Benjamin Netanyahu, who began his talk with the following words:*

> First off, I would like to congratulate the Globes Conference for its foresight in inviting Alan Dershowitz and I would like to say to Alan: Israel has no greater champion and the truth has no greater defender....

Shortly after these flattering words were broadcast on Israeli TV, I received a call on my cell phone from the White House that President Obama wanted to talk to me. I was in a noisy Tel Aviv restaurant when the call came and I couldn't hear much, so I said I would return to my quiet hotel room where I could take the call. An hour or so later, the president called and asked me what three issues were of most concern to the Israelis. I told him that the number one issue was Iran. He asked me what the second issue was and I said Iran. "That's the third, fourth, and fifth issue as well." He invited me to continue the discussion at the White House, which I did several weeks later. We had a long, substantive conversation, during which I expressed deep concern about his administration's policy with regard to the Iranian nuclear weapons program. He was aware of my critical views and he tried to allay my concerns. He assured me that he would never allow Iran to develop nuclear weapons, regardless of what it took, and that no options, including military ones, were off the table. His preference, of course, was for a diplomatic resolution based on a tough sanctions regime that would bring Iran to the bargaining table. But he said that he couldn't be sure that would work and that if it didn't, and if Iran were on the verge of developing a nuclear weapon, he would do whatever had to be done to stop it, including military action. Then he looked me straight in the eye and said: "Alan, you've known me for a long time and you know I don't bluff."

I believed him and left the Oval Office relatively comfortable with his determination to stop Iran from obtaining a nuclear weapon.

Several months later, I was invited to speak to top members of his national security team. In the middle of our substantive discussion, President Obama walked in and said, "Alan, I just want to assure you that nothing has changed from the last time we spoke. Bottom line is that Iran is not going to develop a nuclear weapon. You can count on it."

And I did count on it in making my decision to support President Obama in his reelection campaign against Governor Mitt Romney, who I knew and liked. During the campaign, I wrote a series of articles, which compose this section.

President Obama Turns a Corner on Iran[93]

President Obama has turned an important corner in his efforts to persuade Iran not to try to develop nuclear weapons, and in his efforts to persuade Israel to allow his combination of punishing sanctions and tough talk to work. In his recent interview with Jeffrey Goldberg in *Atlantic* magazine, President Obama sent a clear message to the Iranians that he is not bluffing, that he means it when he says that American policy is not to accept a nuclear Iran, and that no option, including a military one, is off the table if sanctions and threats appear not to be working.

I was not surprised by President Obama's strong words, because he said similar things to me in private conversation. But now he has said them in public, and with words that are unequivocal and put his credibility, and the credibility of our country, on the line. [94]

For those who have claimed that Obama is anti-Israel and/or weak on Iran, these forceful statements should make them reconsider. I, for one, am satisfied with the president's words. Now I want to hear them repeated by Secretary of Defense Leon Panetta, by Joint Chief of Staff Martin Dempsey, and by others in the Obama administration. For me the problem has never been President Obama. His voice has generally been strong and clear in support of Israel's security and his determination to prevent

Iran from securing nuclear weapons. The same cannot be said for other members of his administration. The resulting mixed message has been viewed as a green light, or at the very least a yellow light, by the Iranian mullahs. Now they have been given a clear red light, and if they try to speed past that red light, they should understand the grave consequences.

Having said all this, there still is some distance between the United States and Israel when it comes to timing and red lines. Israel has a closer red line, because it may soon lack the military capacity to destroy Iran's nuclear weapons program if that program succeeds in going underground to bunkers that are impenetrable to Israeli bombs. The United States has more time, and a further red line, because it has far greater capacity to destroy even a deeply buried Iranian nuclear weapons program. This difference requires the Israelis to place great trust in President Obama's promises.

As a nation built on the ashes of the Holocaust, Israel must always heed the lesson Elie Wiesel learned from his horrendous experiences during the Second World War: "Always believe the threats of your enemies more than the promises of your friends."

Israel may feel the need to take its own military action, even if it believes—as it should—that Obama is now expressing his true views and policies regarding a nuclear Iran. Things change. People, even presidents, change their minds. Public attitudes change. Promises are fragile reeds on which to rest life-and-death decisions about one's own population. It is fair to ask the question whether if the shoe were on the other foot, would the United States be willing to put the safety of its citizens in the hands of a close and trusted ally rather than in its own hands. Because the United States has the strongest military in the history of the world, that particular shoe is never on the other foot, yet it is an interesting thought experiment.

I hope, with all my heart, that military action will not be necessary against Iran. As George Washington cautioned in his second inaugural address, "To be prepared for war is one of the most effectual means of preserving peace." A credible threat, backed by extensive military preparation, may be the most effectual means of eliminating the need for a military option.

This is the first time I've been at all optimistic about the possibility that Iran may be frightened into giving up its nuclear weapons program. I never believed that sanctions, regardless of how punishing, would alone work on the Iranian mullahs. But a combination of punishing sanctions and credible threats might just do the job. If not, the military option may become necessary, but it now looks like that option will be held as a sword of Damocles over the heads of the mullahs, rather than being dropped on their heads now. For the sword to work, it must not only hang above their heads, it must be seen by them, and they must believe that we are prepared to have it drop.

B. *Assessing President Obama's Trip*[95]

Now that President Obama is on his way back from his trip to the Middle East, its potential impact can be assessed.* All in all it was a success, despite some pitfalls.

Whenever a high-ranking American dignitary visits Israel, there is concern that something will happen—new settlement building, further rocket attacks—to spoil the visit. It happened again, as President Obama was visiting President Abbas, having had a positive meeting with Prime Minister Netanyahu. This time the spoiler was neither Hamas nor the settlement builders (though rockets were fired and settlements expanded). It was the *New York Times,* running an extensive and illustrated story casting doubt on President Obama's signature gift to Israel: America's financial support for the joint antimissile system called "Iron Dome."

The success of the Iron Dome has been central to Israeli-American relations, as well to the security policies of both countries. An antimissile system capable of destroying up to 90 percent of Hamas rockets directed at Israeli population centers

---

* In mid-March 2013, President Obama visited Israel and Jordan, where he met with various Israeli officials including Prime Minister Netanyahu and President Peres, as well as the president of the Palestinian Authority, Mahmoud Abbas.

has made it possible for Israel to focus on prevention rather than deterrence. This means fewer and shorter counterattacks in Gaza, which translates to fewer casualties on both sides. The success of the antimissile program also promised enhanced protection against Iranian-inspired rocket attacks from Hezbollah, and perhaps even against a potential nuclear attack by Iran (though the technology for deflecting long-range missiles is different than that used to destroy missiles from Gaza and Lebanon).

Along comes the *New York Times* with a devastating and detailed article headlined "Weapons Experts Raise Doubts About Israel's Antimissile System."[96] Experts quoted in the article suggest that the success rate of Iron Dome is a small fraction of that claimed by Israel and the United States—as low as 35 to 40 percent rather than 90 percent. Some experts claim it is even lower than that, which would make it an abject failure rather than the glowing success recently claimed by Vice President Joe Biden and other officials.

Whoever turns out to be correct factually, the perception will now be that Iron Dome is not nearly as effective as claimed. This will embolden Hamas, Hezbollah, and perhaps Iran. It will make Israelis more suspicious of their own government and less appreciative of America's considerable contribution to Iron Dome. It will also create increased insecurities among Israeli citizens who were counting on Iron Dome to protect them.

The timing of the *New York Times* article could not have been worse, coming out right in the midst of President Obama's visit with Israeli and Palestinian leaders and just before his talk to Israeli students. It raised a distracting cloud over his repeated assurances that America will continue to support Israel's security through projects like Iron Dome.

Despite this bad news, there was much good news from the visit. There were reports that President Abbas might be willing to begin negotiations before Israel implemented a settlement freeze, so long as Prime Minister Netanyahu provided private assurances that a freeze would begin after negotiations were under way. This is a slight variation on a proposal I had made to President Abbas back in the fall, to which he had agreed.

President Obama's visit had many goals. His viewing of the Dead Sea Scrolls was intended to emphasize the deep Jewish and Christian relationship to the Land of Israel. His appearance at the tomb of Theodor Herzl was calculated to assure Israelis that during his speech in Cairo, he had not intended to suggest that Zionism began with the Holocaust. His talk to the students manifested his need to speak directly to the Israeli people rather than only to its leaders, because Israel is a vibrant democracy. His casual and warm encounters with Prime Minister Netanyahu and his family were intended to show the world that their relationship is better than how it has been portrayed in the media. All of these symbolic stops achieved their goals.

It remains to be seen, of course, whether the unspoken goals of the trip were achieved: namely, moving the Israeli government and the Palestinian Authority closer to negotiations, and persuading the Israeli leadership that the American approach to preventing Iran from developing nuclear weapons should obviate the need for Israel to act unilaterally in the near future.

President Obama did emphasize the truism that Israel must remain free to take whatever decision it feels necessary to protect itself against a nuclear armed Iran, but I suspect that this green light was openly flashed with the knowledge that Israel has no current plans to take advantage of it. Although differences remain between the red lines laid down by both countries, the two leaders seem closer together on this issue than ever before.

Finally, Obama's approval and trust among Israelis has improved as a result of his media interviews, his talk to the students, his positive approach to Israel's security, and the absence of any demands that Israel make unilateral concessions prior to negotiations. All in all, it was a good beginning, despite the upsetting news about the Iron Dome. What happens next will determine whether there is a happy ending.

c. *J Street Undercuts Obama Policy on Iran*[97]

President Obama recently invited me to the Oval Office for a discussion about Iran. The president reiterated to me in private what he had previously said in public: namely, that he would not allow Iran to develop nuclear weapons; that containment of a nuclear Iran was not an option; that sanctions and diplomatic pressures would be applied and increased first; but that, as a last recourse, the military option would not be taken off the table.

What the president said is now the official American policy with regard to the threat of a nuclear Iran. It is clear that sanctions and diplomacy alone will not convince the Iranian mullahs to halt their progress toward their goal of an Iran with nuclear weapons. The only realistic possibility of persuading the Iranians to give up their nuclear ambitions is for them to believe that there is a credible threat of an American military attack on their nuclear facilities. Unless this threat is credible, the Iranians will persist. And if the Iranians persist, and the Israelis do not believe that the American threat is credible, the Israelis will undertake a military strike against Iranian nuclear facilities. It is crucial, therefore, for America's military threat to be credible and to be perceived as credible by both the Israelis and the Iranians.

Enter J Street. J Street is a lobby in Washington that advertises itself as "pro-Israel and pro-peace." But its policy with regard to Iran is neither pro-Israel nor pro-peace. It is categorically opposed to any "military strike against Iran." It is also opposed to maintaining any credible military threat against Iran, through "legislation authorizing, encouraging, or in other ways laying the groundwork for the use of military force against Iran." This is according to their official policy statement.[98] They favor sanctions and they recognize that "Iran obtaining nuclear weapons would pose a very serious threat to America and Israeli interests." But they believe that diplomacy and sanctions alone can deter Iran from developing nuclear weapons. By advocating this path, they are totally undercutting the policy of the Obama administration. They are sending a message both to Iran and to Israel that there is no credible military threat, and that if Iran is prepared to withstand sanctions and diplomacy, they will have nothing further to worry about if they move forward with their nuclear weapons program.

The Obama administration has tried very hard to persuade Israel that there is no space between the American position and the Israeli position on Iran. Whether or not this is true, there is a hole the size of a nuclear crater between Israel's position, reflecting a widespread consensus within that country, and J Street's position. Virtually every Israeli wants the United States to keep the military option on the table. This includes "doves" such as Israeli President Shimon Peres. Former United States president Bill Clinton also believes that the military option must be maintained. Virtually everyone, Israelis and Americans alike, hopes that the military option will never have to be exercised. But the best way to make sure that it will not have to be exercised is to keep it credible. As George Washington put in his second inaugural speech: "To be prepared for war is one of the most effective means of preserving peace."

J Street, in addition to undercutting both mainstream Israeli and American policies toward Iran, has also mischaracterized the views of those it cites in support of its benighted position. It cites former Mossad chiefs Meir Dagan and Efraim Halevy as opposing any "military strike against Iran." It cites these two Israeli security experts in the context of opposing an American strike and an American threat to strike. Yet Dagan has explicitly stated that he would favor keeping the American military option on the table. This is what he has said: "The military option must always be on the table, with regards to Iran, but it must always be a last option."[99] This is quite different from the misleading manner in which J Street has characterized his views. The same is true of Efraim Halevy. When I read the J Street reference to Halevy, I immediately called him and told him how J Street had characterized his views and asked him if that was a correct characterization. His response: "That's absolutely false." He told me that he had repeatedly stated that the United States must keep the military option on the table as a last resort, though he hoped that it would never have to be used.

J Street can no longer pretend to be pro-Israel, since it is actively seeking to undercut a joint Israeli and American policy designed to protect Israel and the world from a nuclear armed Iran. Nor can J Street claim to be pro-peace, since its policy will likely encourage Iran to take actions that will inevitably result in an attack either by Israel, the United States, or both. Finally, it cannot be trusted to tell the truth, as evidenced by its deliberate misattribution of its views to security experts that don't share them.

Some people have accused J Street of carrying President Obama's water with regard to Israel and of having been "invented" to give the Obama administration cover for taking tough policies with regard to Israeli settlement activity.* But in this instance, J Street is completely undercutting the Obama policy. That would not be so bad except for the fact that the Obama White House sometimes seems to be embracing J Street and its followers. This public embrace sends a message to Iran that the Obama administration may not mean it when it says that it will use military force if necessary to prevent a nuclear armed Iran. This may be a false message, but it is a dangerous one nevertheless. Absolutely no good has come from J Street's soft policy on Iran. Either J Street must change its policy, or truth in advertising requires that it no longer proclaim itself a friend of Israel, a friend of peace, a friend of truth, or a friend of the Obama administration.

---

* By Mr. Ben-Ami's own admission, "Our No. 1 agenda item... is to do whatever we can in Congress to act as the president's blocking back." James Traub, "The New Israel Lobby," *New York Times Magazine*, 9 September 2009

It is now become clear that neither diplomacy nor sanctions will halt the Iranian march toward nuclear weapons. Iran is today stronger diplomatically than it has been in years, as evidenced by the meeting of the nonaligned nations in Tehran. Iran is neither isolated nor alone in a world in which nonaligned nations form a majority at the United Nations.

The sanctions, while hurting the Iranian economy and making life more difficult for the average Iranian, are having zero impact on the Iranian nuclear program, which according to objective intelligence reports is gathering steam and moving even more quickly toward its ultimate goal of a nuclear weapon that will be a game changer. An Iranian nuclear weapon will end any dream of nonproliferation. It will protect Iran's surrogate terrorists, such as Hezbollah, under a formidable nuclear umbrella. And it will make an eventual nuclear war more likely. That is why President Obama rightfully took the containment option off the table and put the preventive military option squarely on it.

Although I support President Obama's policy with regard to the Iranian nuclear threat, I think he must take one further step if the combination of diplomacy and sanctions are ever to work. That step is to communicate to Iran—unequivocally and without any room for misunderstanding—that the Obama administration will *never* allow Iran to develop nuclear weapons.

President Obama has already made this point, but not in a way that the Iranians understand and believe. Language matters, and President Obama must now use language that commits him, in the eyes of the Iranians, to keep his promise that he will, if necessary, use military force to prevent Iran from developing nuclear weapons.

Only if the Iranians truly believe that they will never be allowed to develop nuclear weapons will the combination of diplomacy and sanctions work. The message has to be this: look, sanctions hurt. Diplomatic isolation from first world powers is costly. So why incur this pain and cost if you know you will never be able to achieve your goal?

Not only must the Iranians believe that the United States will, as a last resort, use its overwhelming air power to destroy Iran's nuclear weapons program, but the Israeli leadership must also believe that the Iranians believe it. Only then will Israel forbear from taking preventive self-defense actions on its own.

If the Iranians and the Israelis were to believe President Obama's assurances that, as he put it, "I don't bluff," there would be a real possibility that Iran would abandon its nuclear weapons program. But even if the mullahs were foolishly to challenge the United States and continue with the weapons program, the Israelis would have an enhanced degree of confidence that Obama would keep his word and stop Iran before it reached its deadly goal.

Right now, despite President Obama's best efforts, neither the Iranians nor the Israelis are sufficiently confident that he would carry out his threat. They know that there are those within the administration and among President Obama's supporters who will discourage him from making an unequivocal statement or carrying out a threat, because they believe that sanctions and diplomacy alone will work, without the need for "saber rattling." There are also those who prefer a policy of containment to the threat of military action. The Iranians are aware of this faction and are counting on them to prevail, if it comes down to a choice between allowing Iran to develop nuclear weapons and stopping them by military action. President Obama must make it clear that he has rejected this view and that he will employ military action if that is the only option other than a nuclear Iran.

This is not a debate between peaceniks and warmongers. Every Israeli and American that I know wants peace. Everyone would love to see Iran stop developing nuclear weapons without a rocket being fired or a bomb being dropped. The dispute is about tactics and strategy. President Obama believes that the best way to avoid having to use the military option is to make Iran understand that he will in fact use it as a last alternative to Iran developing the bomb. Those on the other side of this debate believe that making such an unequivocal threat would constitute saber rattling, and that such rattling actually decreases the chance for a peaceful resolution of this difficult issue.

President Obama is right and those who are opposed to his rattling some sabers are wrong. So let President Obama look the mullahs in the eye and persuade them that they simply do not have the option of developing nuclear weapons. The only two options they have are to stop or be stopped. Only if they believe this is there any realistic likelihood that they will stop.

E. *The Message Obama Should Have Sent*[101]

On Monday in New York, Iranian President Mahmoud
Ahmadinejad promised that Israel will be "eliminated," a variation on his previous threats to the nation's existence.[102] He was in
town for the opening of the United Nations General Assembly, a
gathering that reliably sees leaders issuing pronouncements that,
even if not new, at least are given a bigger stage. On Tuesday, the
first day of the gathering, President Obama delivered a speech
that also struck familiar notes, including the statement that "a
nuclear armed Iran is not a challenge that can be contained." He
moved no closer to giving a signal of what he might consider
an intolerable development in Iran's advance toward a nuclear
weapon.

For months, US and Israeli officials have debated whether Mr.
Obama should publicly announce a "red line" that, if crossed by
Iran, would prompt an American military response. Announcing
such a threshold publicly or privately might be helpful, but it may
not be necessary for the president to specify what would constitute such a red line (a certain degree of uranium enrichment,
for example, or other evidence of weaponization).

Instead, Mr. Obama has another good option: tell the Iranian
leadership that under no circumstances will it ever be permitted

to develop or acquire nuclear weapons, and that the US is prepared to take decisive military action to make sure of this.

Such a statement wouldn't tip the president's hand regarding a precise red line, but it would send a clear message that Iran's efforts to develop nuclear weapons are futile and ultimately will lead to disaster for Iran's rulers.

Mr. Obama's prior statements—that containing a nuclear Iran is not an option; that a country committed to wiping Israel off the map, promoting terrorism, and arming Hezbollah and Syria can't be allowed to have nukes—have been strong. But Iran's leadership still doesn't seem to believe that an American military option really is on the table.

Iran's skepticism is understandable in light of some Obama administration rhetoric. This week the president himself characterized Israeli concern over Iran and threats of military action as mere "noise." Defense Secretary Leon Panetta has repeatedly and emphatically outlined the dangers of military action against Iran, and this month Vice President Joe Biden criticized Mitt Romney for being "ready to go to war" with Iran.

Being ready for war with Iran, after all, might be the only way to deter that country from going nuclear.

Were Mr. Obama to affirm America's dedication to blocking Iran's nuclear ambitions through military force if necessary, he would maintain his flexibility to act while putting pressure on Iran's mullahs. He would not be acknowledging, as some fear, that the combination of sanctions and diplomacy is failing. Rather, he would make this combination more effective by convincing Iran's leaders that there is no good reason for them to continue bringing the economic pain of international sanctions onto their country. The message is that their sanctions-provoking projects are pointless because the US will never allow Iran to become a nuclear power.

A policy of sanctions, diplomacy, and an absolute dedication to the use of force if necessary has a far better chance of working than sanctions and diplomacy alone. Sanctions have certainly made life difficult in Iran, at least for the general population, but they haven't slowed the regime's nuclear march. Meanwhile, Israeli leaders have been forced to consider unilateral action in the absence of America's clear commitment to stopping Iran before it's too late.

There are many ways to communicate American preparedness, including by increased military planning and exercises. But there is no substitute for a firm commitment, unambiguously stated by a president whose subordinates do nothing to blur the message and, if anything, signal a steely resolve.

There are those who argue that an American president should never make a threat that he may not want to carry out. But President Obama has already committed his administration to preventing Iran from developing nuclear weapons, which necessarily means employing the military option if all else fails. He has also told the world that he does not bluff. If that is true, then there is no downside to his stating US policy and intentions explicitly.

PART IV.
PRESIDENT OBAMA'S SECOND-TERM POLICY TOWARD IRAN

HAVING BEEN ELECTED *to his final term, President Obama proceeded to make several decisions relating to Iran that caused concern among many of his supporters, especially those who favored a strong policy toward Iran's nuclear program. The first was the appointment of Senator Chuck Hagel to replace Robert Gates as secretary of defense. I expressed my reactions to the appointment in the following article and to other decisions in subsequent articles during his second term.*

President Obama's nomination of Chuck Hagel as secretary of defense risks increasing the likelihood that Iran will develop nuclear weapons.* It poses that risk because Hagel is well known for his opposition both to sanctions against Iran and to employing the military option if necessary.

These views are inconsistent with the very different views expressed by President Obama. The president has emphasized on numerous occasions that he will never allow Iran to develop nuclear weapons and will use military force if necessary to prevent that "game changer."

The nomination of Hagel thus sends a mixed message to the mullahs in Tehran, who will likely interpret it as a change from a red light to a yellow or green one when it comes to their desire to develop nuclear weapons. Sending a mixed message at this point can increase the chances that Iran will miscalculate and act in a foolhardy manner, thus requiring the actual use of the military option—an eventuality that nobody wants.

---

* On 7 January 2013, President Obama nominated Chuck Hagel to serve as his secretary of defense. Despite opposition from many Republicans, including a filibuster, he was eventually confirmed by the Senate on 26 February 2013.

The goal of America's policy toward Iran has always been to frighten the mullahs into believing President Obama's threat to use military force if sanctions fail. "I don't bluff," President Obama has famously and publicly stated. It is imperative that the Iranian leadership believe this. If they do, they may well decide that the sanctions they are currently undergoing are too painful to endure, if the end result is that they will never be permitted to develop nuclear weapons. If they don't believe President Obama's threat, then the sanctions alone will not dissuade them from pursuing their nuclear goal. The nomination of Senator Hagel will strengthen the hand of those within the Iranian leadership who think that President Obama is bluffing.

It is also important that the Israeli leadership believes that President Obama really has Israel's back when it comes to preventing Iran from endangering the Jewish state by obtaining nuclear weapons. Any loss of trust in this regard may result in an Israeli decision to take unilateral military action to protect its citizens against nuclear attacks.

This is the wrong time to send mixed messages by nominating a man who has, at best, a mixed record with regard to sanctions and the military option against Iran and with regard to having Israel's back.

Senator Hagel will have an opportunity to clarify, and hopefully to change, his previous statements with regard to these issues. He should be asked probing questions about sanctions, about the military option, and about Israel's security. In his answers he must persuade the Iranian leadership that there is no distance between his current views and those of the president who has nominated him. The president must also persuade the Iranian leadership that his nomination of Hagel does not constitute any backing down from his commitment to use military force if sanctions don't work.

Independence may be a virtue for a senator, but it is a vice when it presents conflicting messages at a time when it is imperative that the Iranian leadership understand that the Obama administration, indeed the United States as a whole, speaks with one voice when it says that Iran will never be allowed to develop nuclear weapons, even if that requires the use of military force if all other options fail.

Normally a president, especially a president reelected to a second term with a substantial majority, should be entitled to pick his own secretary of defense. But when the president's decision risks sending a mixed message that could increase the chances of having to employ the military option against Iran, the Senate has an especially important role to play. The burden is now on Senator Hagel to persuade the Senate, the American people, and the leaders of Iran that he is fully supportive of the president's commitment not to contain a nuclear armed Iran, but to prevent such a catastrophe from occurring, even if that requires the use of military force to achieve that commendable goal.

Nor is this a liberal-conservative or Democratic-Republican issue. Reportedly, the Hagel nomination has been very controversial within the White House itself, with some of President Obama's closest advisers being critical of it. Many Democrats, both elected officials and rank and file voters, are deeply concerned about the wisdom of the president's nomination of Senator Hagel. Neither is this an issue that concerns only Jewish or pro-Israel voters. There are serious policy issues at stake here. Those of us who voted for President Obama and who want to be certain that Iran is never allowed to develop nuclear weapons, as the president promised, have legitimate concerns about this nomination. We hope that these concerns can be allayed by the president and his nominee, but if they are not, it will be the highest of patriotic duties to oppose Senator Hagel's nomination.

Congressional approval for a punitive-deterrent strike against Syria's use of chemical weapons should not be misunderstood by Iran, Israel, or anyone else. The decision, which involved many moving parts, was not intended to show any weakened resolve to prevent Iran from developing nuclear weapons. Nor was it intended to represent any American trend toward increasing isolationism, either in relation to the world in general or the Middle East in particular.

The president's decision to take his case to Congress was the result of a complex of reasons, both constitutional and political. It was made by a president who had campaigned on the principle that congressional approval for nonemergency military actions is generally desirable and sometimes legally required. But it was also made by a president who had committed our nation to a red line that, if crossed, would demand a response.

Hence the conflict: a president cannot commit his nation to a red line if he is also committed to securing congressional approval before responding to the crossing of that red line. What if Congress denies approval? Must the president still keep his red line commitment? If he does not, what does this say about other red line commitments, such as that made regarding Iran's efforts to secure nuclear weapons? How will Iranian mullahs interpret the president's decision to go to Congress? And how will the Israeli government respond to it? Will misunderstandings increase the likelihood of a military confrontation with Iran? These questions and the uncertainty of the answers reflect the dilemma posed by the president's decision to go to Congress after drawing a red line that Syria has crossed.

There is a way out of this dilemma, at least with regard to Iran and its future actions. The president should secure congressional approval now as to the red line with Iran.

President Obama should ask Congress for authorization now to take military action against Iran's nuclear weapons program if it were to cross the red line he has already drawn. If Congress gives its approval, that action will increase the deterrent threat currently directed against Iran by underscoring the red line as having been drawn both by the president and by Congress. It should leave no doubt in the minds of the Iranian mullahs that the president not only has the will to enforce the red line but also has the authority from Congress to do so.

Having the authority to engage in military action does not require that the president take such action; it only empowers him to do so if he chooses, without further action by Congress. But as President Obama has repeatedly warned: he does not bluff; if he says he will not permit Iran to develop nuclear weapons, he means it—unless Congress stops him. If Congress were now to give advance approval to the red line with Iran, the mullahs will understand that there will be no stopping the president from keeping his word. Only if the mullahs believe that President Obama will attack their nuclear reactors if they cross the red line will there be any hope of deterring them from doing so. The goal is not to have the president actually attack Iran. It is to persuade Iran that he will do so if they defy the will of Congress, the president, and the American people by crossing the red line.

President Obama has already shown Iran that he is willing to take military action against Syria without the approval of the UN Security Council, Great Britain, NATO, the Arab League, and other representatives of the international community—as long as he has the approval of Congress. This is especially important with regard to Iran, because Congress is more likely to support military action against Iran's nuclear weapons program than is the international community.

There are dangers in drawing red lines too far in advance of them being crossed. A president who commits his nation to taking action if the line is crossed ties his hands, as the events in Syria demonstrate. But President Obama has already tied his hands on Iran—and properly so. He has made a commitment not only to the American people, whose national security would be placed at risk by a nuclear armed Iran, but also to the leaders of Jordan, Saudi Arabia, the Emirates, and Israel, for whom a nuclear armed Iran poses an even greater threat. And Israel has acted—or forborne from acting—in reliance on that firm commitment. Now these American allies must be assured— and America's enemies, especially Iran, must be warned—that President Obama is capable of keeping his promise, and that Congress won't stop him from doing so.

Iran is different from Syria. America's national interest would be directly weakened if Iran were to develop nuclear weapons. It has not been directly weakened by Assad's use of chemical weapons against his own people. The case for a red line against Iran is far stronger than it was for a red line against Syria.

Congress should first authorize the president to keep his commitment with regard to Syria. Then it should authorize the president to keep his far more important commitment with regard to the red line against Iran. This dual congressional action will strengthen America's position in the world and will help to prevent the game-changing disaster of a nuclear armed Iran.

How the New York Times Distorted Netanyahu's UN Speech[105]

I was in the General Assembly when Israeli Prime Minister Benjamin Netanyahu delivered his speech about Iranian President Hassan Rohani and Iran's nuclear program. I heard a very different speech from the one described by the *New York Times* and other media. Not surprisingly, the Iranians described it as "inflammatory." More surprisingly, the *New York Times* described Netanyahu's speech as aggressive, combative, sarcastic, and sabotaging diplomacy, while the only expert it quoted called the speech ineffective and pushing the limits of credibility.

What I heard in the assembly bore little relationship either to the Iranian or the *New York Times* characterizations. What the people at the talk heard was a compellingly persuasive speech using Rohani's own words to prove convincingly that his friendly smile is a cover for far more malignant intentions. Herein are a few excerpts not quoted in the *Times* report. First, with regard to Iran's nuclear weapons program:

> There are those who would readily agree to leave Iran with a residual capability to enrich uranium. I advise them to pay close attention to what Rohani said in his

speech to Iran's... Supreme Cultural Revolutionary Council. This was published in 2005. I quote:...

> "A county that could enrich uranium to about 3.5 percent will also have the capability to enrich it to about 90 percent. Having fuel cycle capability virtually means that a country that possesses this capability is able to produce nuclear weapons."

Precisely. This is why Iran's nuclear weapons program must be fully and verifiably dismantled. And this is why the pressure on Iran must continue.

Next, several statements Rohani made withregard to human rights, terrorism, and constructive engagement:

Rohani spoke of, quote, "the human tragedy in Syria." Yet, Iran directly participates in Assad's murder and massacre of tens of thousands of innocent men, women, and children in Syria. And that regime is propping up a Syrian regime that just used chemical weapons against its own people.

Finally, Netanyahu's answer to Rohani's assurance that his country does not engage in deceit and secrecy:

> Last Friday Rohani assured us that in pursuit of its nuclear program, Iran—this is a quote—Iran has never chosen deceit and secrecy, never chosen deceit and secrecy. Well, in 2002 Iran was caught red-handed secretly building an underground centrifuge facility in Natanz. And then in 2009 Iran was again caught red-handed secretly building a huge underground nuclear facility for uranium enrichment in a mountain near Qom.

Nor did Netanyahu reject diplomacy. Indeed he welcomed it, so long as the diplomatic solution "fully dismantles Iran's nuclear weapons program and prevents it from having one in the future."

The *New York Times* was particularly critical of Netanyahu's oft-repeated statement that if Iran were to be on the verge of developing nuclear weapons designed to wipe Israel off the map, "against such a threat Israel will have no choice but to defend itself." But this statement reflects not only Israel's longstanding policy but American policy as well. President Obama has told me, as he has told others, that Israel must reserve the right to take military action in defense of its own civilian population. It cannot be expected, any more than we can be expected, to outsource the ultimate obligation of every democracy to protect its citizens from nuclear attack. During the Cuban Missile Crisis, President John F. Kennedy made it clear that the United States would not accept nuclear weapons pointed at our cities from bases in Cuba. Does anybody really expect Israel to accept nuclear missiles directed at its cities and towns from an even more belligerent enemy sworn to its destruction?

Those of us who were in the General Assembly chamber to hear Netanyahu's speech heard a rational call for diplomacy backed by sanctions and the ultimate threat of military force as a last resort. It heard the leader of America's ally, Israel, carefully analyze the words and deeds of the leader of a nation that still describes the United States in the most bellicose of terms. It was one of the most compelling and effective speeches ever delivered at the United Nations. It should be read—or watched on YouTube—by every American, who should then compare what they have seen and heard with what the media told them was said.

Several media outlets misinterpreted President Rohani's speech to make it sound far more acceptable than it would have been had it been correctly translated. The media claimed that Farsi is a difficult language to translate. There was no such excuse with regard with Prime Minister Netanyahu's speech, which was delivered in crystal clear English. The distortion of the Israeli prime minister's speech was a deliberate attempt to portray him in a less favorable manner than his actual words warranted.

The question remains: Why would the American media bend over forward to place Rohani in a positive light while bending over backward to present Netanyahu in a negative light? Is it because we place our understandable hope for peace over the reality that difficult barriers that still exist? Is it because a "friendly" Iranian head of state is a more interesting story than a realistic Israeli head of state?

Whatever the reason, distorting reality is neither in the interest of good reporting nor in the interest of peace. If diplomacy is to succeed, it must be based on real politicking and a hardnosed assessment of both our friends and our enemies. Judged against those standards, the media reporting on the Rohani and Netanyahu speeches did not meet the high standards rightly expected of American journalism.

D. *Oppose the Deal on Iran*[106]

The deal that has been offered to Iran—to soften some sanctions in return for a promise by the mullahs to preserve the status quo with regard to their nuclear program—does not serve the interest of peace. This is not to discourage further diplomacy and negotiations, but it is to underline what Secretary of State John Kerry has said: namely that a bad deal is worse than no deal. This is a very bad deal for America, its allies, and peace.

Diplomacy is better than war, but bad diplomacy can cause bad wars. The US is leading the noble efforts, stalled for the moment, to achieve a diplomatic breakthrough in our determination to prevent Iran from developing, or having the capacity to develop, nuclear weapons. There is little dispute about this essential goal: virtually everyone agrees that a nuclear armed Iran would pose unacceptably grave dangers to the United States and its allies.

Nor is there much controversy over the preference for "jaw jaw" over "war war" as Winston Churchill once put it. But the understandable concern, expressed by Israeli, French, Saudi, and some other leaders, is that the Iranian leadership is playing for time—that they want to make insignificant concessions in exchange for significant reductions in the sanctions that are crippling their economy. Their goal is to have their yellow cake and eat good food at the same time. These leaders, and many experienced nuclear and diplomatic experts, fear that a bad deal, such as the one that Secretary Kerry seemed ready to accept, would allow the Iranians to inch closer to nuclear weapons capacity while strengthening their faltering economy. The net result would be a more powerful Iran with the ability to deploy a nuclear arsenal quickly and surreptitiously.

Were this to occur, we would be witnessing a recurrence of the failed efforts to prevent a nuclear North Korea but in a far more volatile and dangerous neighborhood of the globe. Were Iran to use the current diplomatic efforts as a cover to buy time to make a preventive military attack unrealistic, this would indeed be our "Chamberlain moment," a replication of the time three-quarters of a century ago when the idealistic but naive British prime minister made a bad deal with the Nazis in a desperate but futile effort to avoid deploying the military option against Hitler's growing power.

Winston Churchill, despite his preference for jaw, railed against Chamberlain's concession, describing it as a defeat without a war. The war, of course, soon came, and the allies were in a weaker position, having ceded the industrially and militarily critical Sudetenland to Germany while at the same time giving it more time to enhance its military power. The result was tens of millions of deaths that might have been avoided if the British and French had engaged in a preventive war instead of giving dangerous concessions to the Nazis when they were still weak.

The immediate choice for the world today is not between diplomacy and preventive war, as it may have been in 1938. We have a third option: to maintain or even increase the sanctions while keeping the military option on the table. It was this powerful combination that brought a weakened and frightened Iran to the bargaining table in the first place. It is this combination that will pressure them to abandon their unnecessary quest for nuclear weapons, if anything will. To weaken the sanction regime now, in exchange for a promise to maintain the status quo, would be bad diplomacy, poor negotiation, and a show of weakness precisely when a show of strength is called for.

The leadership of the pro-Israel community, both in the United States and Israel, has shown rare unity around the issue of not weakening the sanctions merely in exchange for the promise of a nuclear standstill from the Iranians. Liberals and conservatives, doves and hawks, all seem to realize that the best way to avoid the Scylla and Charybdis of a nuclear Iran or a military attack is to maintain the tough sanctions while diplomacy continues.

As usual, the only outlier seems to be J Street, whose claim to be pro-Israel grows less credible by the day. Previously, J Street claimed to support tough sanctions as an alternative to the military option and drumbeating. But now that Israel and its supporters insist that sanctions be maintained, J Street seems to be supporting the Neville Chamberlain approach to diplomacy: make substantial concessions in exchange for hollow promises, thereby weakening our negotiating position and increasing the chances that the United States will be forced to take military action as the only means of preventing Iran from developing nuclear weapons.

This is the time when the entire pro-Israel community must stand together in opposition to the deal being offered the Iranians—a deal that is bad for the United States, for the West, and for Israel. The Israeli people seem united in opposition to this bad deal. The American Congress is doubtful about the deal. This is not a liberal/conservative issue. Liberals who view military action as a last resort should oppose this deal, and conservatives who fear a nuclear Iran above all else should oppose this deal.

Indeed all reasonable, thinking people should understand that weakening the sanctions against Iran without demanding that they dismantle their nuclear weapons program is a prescription for disaster. Have we learned nothing from North Korea and Neville Chamberlain?

E. *Congress Must Keep the Military Option on the Table*[107]

The Obama administration's preference for diplomacy with Iran over military action is commendable. There is a chance that diplomacy may even achieve more than sanctions. This possibility lies at the root of the deal recently undertaken with regard to Iran's nuclear program.

No one knows for certain whether Iran is for real when it promises never to seek or develop any nuclear weapons in exchange for an end to sanctions and to its international isolation. No one knows for sure whether there is an internal struggle going on within Iran in which that issue is being debated and considered. No one knows for sure whether the deal recently signed will encourage those who favor ending Iran's quest for nuclear weapons (if there are any such) or whether it will strengthen hardliners who are simply playing for time. The only certainty is that we are uncertain about the true Iranian motivations underlying its willingness to enter into negotiations and to freeze its nuclear program for six months in exchange for a reduction in sanctions.

Diplomacy under conditions of uncertainty always entails risks on all sides. The United States is prepared to take the risk because it has far less to lose if it turns out to be wrong. Israel and Saudi Arabia are unwilling to shoulder the risk because they have so much more to lose if the American assessment turns out to be wrong.

Many American experts—diplomatic, nuclear, political, economic—believe that even the risks to the United States exceed the benefits, and that accordingly this was a bad deal for our country. Others disagree. The important point is that this is not only a dispute between the US and Israel, as some seem to be characterizing it. It is a hotly disputed issue within the US, within the Democratic Party, among nuclear experts, and within the diplomatic establishment.

Nor should this be seen by those who oppose the deal, as I do, as a demonstration of bad faith on the part of the Obama administration toward Israel. This a reasonable disagreement between friends as to the best course of action, both over the short and long terms. The stakes, however, are exceedingly high for Israel, because it cannot afford for the US to be wrong in its assessment and balancing of the acknowledged risks.

I think the United States is wrong because I believe that the supreme leader of Iran is determined to secure the ability to obtain nuclear weapons in its quest for hegemony over the Middle East. I do not believe that the smiling face of its newly elected (with the approval of the supreme leader) president reflects the attitude of the current Iranian leadership. I also believe that one of the goals of the Iranian leadership is to drive a deep wedge between the United States and its allies in the Middle East, especially Israel and Saudi Arabia. This deal has helped to do that.

Now that the six-month clock has begun to tick, what can be done to make the best out of a dangerous situation? First, Congress can hang two swords of Damocles over the neck of Iran.

It can now authorize the president to take military action in the event that Iran breaks its part of the deal and secretly begins to move toward developing nuclear weapons. Second, it can legislate harsh sanctions that would automatically go into effect if it became clear that Iran was simply buying time and had no interest in halting its nuclear weapons program.

The Iranians came to the negotiating table only because of a combination of harsh sanctions and a realistic military option. Both of these sticks must be kept on the table if the carrot of reduced sanctions is to have any possibility of working.

Israel too must maintain its military pressure on Iran, and the US should make it clear that if Israel were to feel the need to deploy its military option as a last resort, it could count on American support.

These are tense and dangerous times. The risks on all sides are considerable. This is the time for allies to stick together and not to allow their differences to create the kind of wedge that Iran seeks to encourage and exploit. Unless there is a concerted commitment to prevent Iran from developing a nuclear weapon capacity, the end result will replicate the North Korean model, where the facade of diplomacy was used as a cover by North Korea to develop nuclear weapons.

If Iran ends up using this deal to help it develop nuclear weapons, the result would be a game changer that could cause a catastrophe. An Iran armed with nuclear weapons must be prevented at all costs, as President Obama has promised to do. We must keep our word and keep the military option on the table if diplomacy fails, as it may well do. The only thing more dangerous than a military attack against Iran's nuclear weapons program would be a nuclear armed Iran.

F. *A Discussion with the Pilot Who Bombed the Iraqi Nuclear Reactor*

On 11 December 2013 I was invited to speak at an event hosted by the Institute for National Security Studies in Tel Aviv, titled "Legality and Legitimacy: An Evening with Professor Alan Dershowitz." The event, which was moderated by Pnina Sharvit Baruch, the former head of the International Law Department of the Israel Defense Forces, featured remarks by Elyakim Rubinstein, a justice of the Israeli Supreme Court; former Israeli Justice Minister Tzipi Livni; and a discussion with Amos Yadlin, the former Chief of Staff of the Israeli Air Force, Air Intelligence Directorate, and one of the eight pilots who bombed Iraq's Osirak nuclear reactor in 1981. I have included excerpts of this conversation in the following chapter, and made minor modifications for clarity.

ALAN DERSHOWITZ: Let me begin by commending President Obama and Secretary Kerry for trying to have a diplomatic approach. We all know that diplomacy is preferred to war. Even Winston Churchill, who certainly understood the risks of diplomatic resolutions of the kind Chamberlain accepted, said, "*Jaw, jaw* is better than *war, war*."

The goal is to bring about a cessation of Iran's nuclear weapons program, without a shot having to be fired. The end result is to bring Iran into the international community, to have them end their support for Hezbollah, and to stop them from being a rogue nation. I think there is about a 10 percent chance of that happening. President Obama thinks there is a fifty-fifty chance. The one thing we know as an absolute certainty is that we know nothing with absolute certainty about Iran's state of mind. We are guessing. We don't know whether or not the Supreme Leader of Iran has put a president in the front with the nice smiling face in order to conceal from the world his intentions to develop nuclear weapons aimed at Israel, to create a nuclear umbrella under which terrorism can operate, and to hold a sword of Damocles over Israel to encourage many people to leave for fear of a possible nuclear attack.

There are two other possible scenarios: one, the Supreme Leader has changed his mind and understands that the United States and Israel have given him the option either to end the nuclear program or lose his regime. And he thought he would prefer not to lose his regime and so he has changed his mind. Then, I think there is a second possibility: that there is an internal struggle going on in Iran. The revolutionary guard seems to be critical of the deal but there are some elements within Iran that are favorable. There was some popular uprising in the street, so, maybe, there is a process going on. The question then would be how best to influence that process in the right direction, whether by maintaining the sanctions, increasing the sanctions, maintaining a credible military threat, or making a deal of the kind that was made. My view is that maintaining the military option and keeping the sanctions is a better way of influencing that outcome than the deal we have now made.* I think Iran has gotten what they want from the deal, namely the beginning of the end of the sanctions process.

What have they had to give up in exchange? They haven't had to give up the building of rockets, which are capable of carrying nuclear weapons. You might ask, why are they developing rockets capable of carrying nuclear weapons if they deny having a nuclear weapons program? The Iranians see this as a victory. The difference is not between American and Israeli intelligence assessments; I think the intelligence assessments are essentially the same. I think the big difference is that America is many thousands of miles away and not at immediate risk; therefore it can place hope over fear. Israel is so close and is the intended target of any nuclear program, so it has to place fear over hope. How one stands on the threat of a nuclear program depends on where one sits in relation to the threat. Having said that, I think the potential for failure is greater than the potential for success. Now we should start looking forward and see what the United States and Israel can do together to increase the possibility of a good deal. After all, one of Iran's goals was to create a gulf between Israel and the United States. There has been criticism by Israel, but the White House may appreciate that Israel acting as the "bad cop" by being critical of the United States may help the United States in its negotiating posture. The question is one of degree. So I think right now the issue is how to narrow the gulf and get the least worst deal.

---

*   The "deal" in this discussion refers to the six-month agreement reached on 24 November 2013 between the P5+1 and Iran to halt Iran's nuclear program temporarily. The agreement was subsequently extended: see Appendix 1 for further details.

My fear is that the Obama administration may have a different goal than Israel in the long term: that is, that the Obama administration might be satisfied by kicking the can to make sure that Iran doesn't develop a nuclear weapon on President Obama's watch. I sat next to President Obama and he said: "Alan, you've known me for a long time. I don't bluff, I am telling you." Looking me in the eye, he said: "Iran will not develop a nuclear bomb on my watch. I have Israel's back." And he was very clear about that and I was very clear in saying: "Mr. President, I believe that you believe that *now*. No one can know what you may believe in a year or in two years when Iran gets close and the decision has to be made. Who knows what sabers will be rattled by China, or by Russia. You may not be in a position to keep that promise, and that is why you can't ask Israel to outsource the defense of its civilians to another country."

It is essential to keep the military option on the table, particularly a joint military option between the United States and Israel. We all hope that the military option does not have to be deployed. Right now Iran does not believe there is a military option. Right now Iran's state of mind is that America will not employ the military option, that Israel needs the green light from the United States to deploy it and that Israel will not get that green light. I don't believe Israel thinks it needs a green light from the United States.

The next years are going to be crucial in the history of American-Israel relations, in the history of Israel, and in the history of Israel's relations with Iran.

AMOS YADLIN: Before you deploy the military option, you have to ask four fundamental questions. First, can you do it? Second, what is more dangerous for Israel: an Iran with the bomb, or bombing Iran and there will be an Iranian reaction? If you conclude that the bomb is most dangerous, then you have to consider what Israel can legitimately do. Finally, you have to ask what is the opinion of your greatest ally, sometimes your only ally, the US. You are absolutely right, we never ask for a green light. If we feel that we have to do it, we will do it. But if the red light is burning here, it is a serious consideration.

About the agreement itself, the agreement is not necessarily all bad. For the first time after ten years, the Iranians are stopping the program. If they are now four to six months from the bomb, they will be going backward a week, but they are not going forward. And there will be a better inspection and the sanction regime according to those who signed the agreement. So this is the good news. The bad news is that they got permission to enrich. Contrary to the United Nations Security Council resolutions—four of them. It basically told them it is not the PM of Israel that told them to stop all enrichment. It is the United Nations Security Council resolutions. This agreement hasn't touched anything to do with the military dimension of the program, that the Iranians do not admit exists, but we all know it exists. And there is, of course, the danger that the permanent agreement will solve the problems of everyone except Israel. The Iranians will be happy; the Americans will be happy. The Prime Minister said it's a very bad deal. I said it is an acceptable deal for six months, but if it becomes a comprehensive deal, it is a very bad deal. Last but not least, I agree that we now have to put this agreement behind us and work very hard on the parameters of the comprehensive agreement—and if this agreement has stopped the Iranians, and took them back a week, a month, back from the bomb, we have to take them back years from the bomb. And this can be done only if all the activities they are doing today that are aimed at a military nuclear bomb are eliminated and anything they will be given will be civilian. We may lose the only two leverages that we have against the Iranians, and this is a very tough sanction regime, and a credible military option.

ALAN DERSHOWITZ: Dean Acheson once said that no country's survival has ever been made to depend on international law. International law in this regard is somewhat anachronistic—it is out of date. In fact, it was never viable. Let me give you an example. If Great Britain had made a decision in 1937 to attack Nazi Germany because they were building up an arms system capable of destroying all of Europe, they would have been in violation of international law, and yet it would have been the right thing to do. And the United States when it had mutually assured destruction with the Soviet Union as its Cold War goal— if you bomb New York, we will bomb Moscow—was a violation of international law. You are not allowed to bomb civilian targets in retaliation for the bombing of your own civilian targets. Continuing with the example: if Churchill had been the Prime Minister in 1937, and ordered an attack that had killed the entire Nazi regime, destroyed the entire Nazi party, and in the process killed 10,000 innocent German civilians, he would have gone down in history as a butcher, a barbarian, and a paradigm of the violation of international law. And yet, he would have saved 50 million lives. Yet nobody would have known that, because history is blind, deaf, and dumb. It doesn't understand contingencies; it doesn't understand the future. It doesn't understand what would happen if Israel or the United States were to take the decision as a last resort to destroy Iran's nuclear weapons. Nobody could know what it would have prevented. That is not an argument for doing it.

Remember that Article 51 of the UN Charter wouldn't even have permitted Israel to attack preemptively in 1967. As a result of Israel's attack in 1967, and other factors, the United Nations appointed a commission to re-look at Article 51 and they said that preemptive wars are justified under international law, in violation of the language of the article. They said as to preventive wars, it is a very hard question, but if it comes to nuclear weapons and your survival, at least you can make the case for it. Now, the argument that international law would prohibit an attack because they don't have a bomb is not recognizing that you cannot attack a country once it has a nuclear bomb. Look at North Korea. Look at Pakistan. If you are going to attack a nuclear weapons program, it must be done before the nuclear weapon is developed; otherwise you will cause enormous environmental damage.

I cannot imagine any rational government making a decision on its own survival based on academics in the Sorbonne deciding what international law should be in a society of perfect beings. If men and women were angels, we would not need law. Today we need an international organization that recognizes that some people are evil and intend to do great harm if they are not deterred or prevented from carrying out their evil intentions.

G. *The Education of a Wartime President*[108]

Last year the Obama administration issued, with considerable fanfare, a new military policy designed to reduce civilian casualties when US forces are attacking enemy targets. This policy required "near certainty" that there will be no civilian casualties before an air attack is permitted.

When Israel acted in self-defense this summer against Hamas rocket and tunnel attacks, the Obama administration criticized the Israeli army for "not doing enough" to reduce civilian casualties. When pressed about what more Israel could do—especially when Hamas fired its rockets and dug its terror tunnels in densely populated areas, deliberately using humans as shields—the Obama administration declined to provide specifics.

Now the Obama administration has exempted itself from its own "near certainty" standard in its attacks against Islamic State, also known as ISIS, in Iraq and Syria. In a statement on 30 September responding to questions by Michael Isikoff at Yahoo News, the administration said that in fighting Islamic State, the US military can no longer comply with Mr. Obama's vow last year to observe "the highest standard we can meet."

The statement came after a Tomahawk missile last week struck the village Kafr Daryan in Syria, reportedly killing and injuring numerous civilians, including children and women. The missile was directed at Al Qaeda terrorists that the White House calls the Khorasan Group, but apparently the Tomahawk hit a home for displaced civilians. The Pentagon says it is investigating the incident, but YouTube video of injured children and the appearance by angry Free Syria Army rebel commanders at a congressional hearing about the attack—an attack that prompted protests in several Syrian villages—left little doubt about what happened.

If this sounds familiar, it is because in every attack on terrorists who operate from civilian areas, there will be civilian casualties. This is especially so when terrorists employ a policy of hiding behind civilian human shields in order to confront their enemies with a terrible choice: not attack a legitimate military target, or attack it and likely cause civilian casualties, which the terrorists can then exploit in the war of public opinion.

Hamas has employed this approach effectively in its periodic wars against Israel. Hamas fighters fire rockets at Israeli civilian targets from densely populated areas near United Nations facilities, mosques, hospitals, and private homes. These areas, rather than the less densely populated open areas between the cities of Gaza, are intentionally selected. Hamas urges civilians to stand on the roofs of buildings that are used to store rockets and that serve as command-and-control shelters.

The fighters dare Israel to attack these shielded military targets. Israel responds by issuing warnings—by leaflets, telephone, and noise bombs—to the civilians, urging them to leave. When civilians try to leave, Hamas fighters sometimes force them back at gunpoint. The fighters launch their missiles using a time delay, giving themselves the opportunity to hide in tunnels where only they are allowed to seek shelter; civilians are left exposed to Israel's efforts to destroy the rockets.

When Israel does attack military targets such as a rocket launcher or a tunnel entrance, and kills or injures civilians, Hamas operatives stand ready to exploit the dead for the international media, who are ever ready to show the victims without mentioning that they died because Hamas was using them as human shields.

Now ISIS and other jihadists in Iraq and Syria are beginning to emulate the Hamas strategy, embedding fighters in towns and villages, thus making military strikes difficult without risking civilian casualties. That is why the Obama administration has exempted itself from its theoretical "near certainty" policy, which has proved to be unworkable and unrealistic in actual battle conditions involving human shields and enemy fighters embedded in densely populated areas.

For the US, the fight against ISIS is a war of choice. Islamic State fighters pose no immediate and direct threat to the American homeland. For Israel, by contrast, Hamas poses an immediate and direct threat. Both the US and Israel seek to minimize civilian casualties. Neither can do so under an unrealistic principle of "near certainty."

Israel has come closer to this high theoretical standard than have the United States and its various coalition partners—for instance, only Israel would employ small rooftop "knock-knock" explosives to warn civilians of a coming missile strike. Yet Israel is the only nation that is routinely condemned by the United Nations, the international community, the media, the academy, and even the US for "not doing enough," in Mr. Obama's words, to reduce civilian casualties. As the president is learning, war is hell. The possibility of waging it with "near certainty" of anything is a chimera.

There must be a single universal standard for judging nations that are fighting the kind of terrorism represented by ISIS and Hamas. The war against ISIS provides an appropriate occasion for the international community to agree on a set of standards that can be applied across the board. These standards must be both moral and realistic, capable of being applied equally to the US, to Israel, and to all nations committed both to the rule of law and to the obligation to protect citizens from terrorist attacks.

The decision of the Obama administration to abandon its unrealistic "highest standard" pledge indicates the urgent need to revisit anachronistic rules with which no nation can actually comply, but against which only one nation—Israel—is repeatedly judged.

H. *Why Is the Obama Administration Provoking Israel?*[109]

A senior Obama administration official recently went on the record with journalist Jeffrey Goldberg in calling Prime Minister Benjamin Netanyahu a "chickenshit." A second senior official also went on the record calling Netanyahu a "coward" on the issue of Iran's nuclear threat.[110]

If these reports are accurate, the following question must be asked: did the Obama administration—indeed perhaps President Barack Obama himself—authorize two senior officials to issue these highly provocative and challenging statements? The White House has now tried to distance itself from the views expressed by these individuals, but it seems unlikely that two senior administration officials would go on the record using such explosive words without White House approval.

The author of the report, Jeffrey Goldberg, tells us that this is the way American and Israeli officials now talk about each other "behind closed doors." But these statements were not made behind closed doors. They were made to a prominent journalist, with the intention of having them published and read not only by American and Israeli officials, but also by Iranian officials.

That question becomes particularly important in light of another quotation attributed to one of the senior officials: "It's too late for him to do anything [regarding a military strike on Iran's nuclear facilities]. Two, three years ago, this was a possibility. But ultimately he couldn't bring himself to pull the trigger. It was a combination of our pressure and his own unwillingness to do anything dramatic. Now it's too late."

That official added: "The feeling now is that Bibi's [Netanyahu] bluffing... he's not Begin at Osirak."

This disclosure of such classified administration assessments—whether true or false—will certainly be welcomed in Tehran. It strengthens the Iranian bargaining position, and weakens the power of the United States to demand more of Iran in the ongoing nuclear negotiations and to demand more of our allies in the event these negotiations break down and additional sanctions are needed.

Goldberg acknowledges that "the Obama administration used the threat of an Israeli strike in a calculated way to convince its allies (and some of its adversaries) to line up behind what turned out to be an effective sanctions regime." By now revealing its belief that there is no longer a real threat of an Israeli strike—again, whether their assessment is correct or incorrect—these senior officials have done considerable damage to security of the United States and to the possibility of striking an effective deal with Iran.

The bottom-line result of these disclosures by two senior Obama officials is to make it more likely that Iran will develop nuclear weapons. Revealing intelligence assessments that suggest Netanyahu is bluffing can only encourage the Iranians to move forward more quickly with their nuclear weapons program.

It also encourages them to believe that the United States will no longer be able to use the threat of an Israeli military strike to shore up support among reluctant allies to increase or even maintain sanctions.

Why then were these officials sent out to talk to Jeffrey Goldberg? By whom were they sent? And why now? If they were not authorized to make these statements and took it upon themselves to do so, they should be fired. That is the only way to send a powerful message to friend and foe alike that the views they expressed do not represent those of the president. If they are not fired, then Congress should ask why two senior Obama administration officials have endangered American national security by increasing the likelihood that Iran will develop nuclear weapons. President Obama has himself acknowledged that a nuclear armed Iran would be a "game changer" that would directly endanger our national security.

Congress has an obligation to get to the bottom of this foreign policy mess. It need not subpoena the journalist, who will surely invoke reportorial privilege. But it can subpoena the handful of senior Obama administration officials who might have made these disclosures. Once Congress establishes who the two senior officials are, they can be asked whether the disclosures were authorized, and if so, by whom.

The president may well invoke executive privilege, but Congress's need to know who is undercutting American foreign policy, and why, should trump any claim of privilege. No administration should have the right to leak damaging information to America's enemies and then hide behind privilege to prevent Congress from learning the source of the leaks and the reasoning, if any, behind the decision to disclose such damaging information.

Beyond the damage done with regard to Iran is the damage done to United States–Israel relations by the insulting and demeaning words used by senior Obama administration officials to describe the prime minister of a close ally. Benjamin Netanyahu fought bravely for his country in one of Israel's most elite and dangerous military units. He has rescued hostages, defended his country against terrorists, and lost a brother at Entebbe.

To call him a "chickenshit" or a "coward" is beneath contempt. Having seen the heavy cost of warfare, he has always been cautious and prudent about committing Israeli troops to battle. For this he should be praised rather than condemned.

Netanyahu may soon have to make an existential decision about whether to allow Iran to develop nuclear weapons that might be used against Israeli citizens or to authorize a dangerous military attack designed to destroy and delay Iran's capacity to develop such weapons of mass destruction. This decision would be difficult for any leader, and it is even more difficult for a leader of a tiny country surrounded by enemies and isolated by much of the international community. To trivialize and reduce this decision to name-calling words like "chickenshit" and "coward" demonstrates extraordinary bad judgment on the part of those who used the words and those who may have authorized their use.

There are legitimate and important differences between the Obama and Netanyahu administrations over issues such as building in Jerusalem and the stalled peace negotiations.

Each side has criticized the other's position on their merits and demerits. But scatological name-calling on the record has no place in an alliance between friends.

Those responsible for these provocative and dangerous ad hominems and for the unwarranted disclosure of classified intelligence assessments must be held accountable by the American public and by all those who care about peace in the Middle East.

1. *Will the Newly Elected Congress Push Obama into Being Tougher on Iran's Nuclear Weapons Program?*[111]

Now that both houses of Congress are controlled by the GOP, will President Obama have as free a hand in making a deal with the Iranian mullahs regarding their nuclear weapons program?

Many members of Congress, in both chambers and on both sides of the aisle, believe that President Obama is willing to allow Iran to become a threshold nuclear weapons power as long as it doesn't actually develop a nuclear bomb during his watch. Israeli leaders, both in the majority and in opposition, fear the same thing. Nobody wants to see a nuclear armed Iran, and few want to see a military attack on Iran's nuclear weapons program, except as an absolute last resort. Everyone would like to see a good deal that assures the world that Iran will never develop nuclear weapons, and in return for that assurance ends the crippling sanctions against the Iranian people. The questions are what sort of a deal will bring us closer to this desirable outcome, and are the United States and its European allies demanding enough from Iran to assure compliance with a commitment not to weaponize its "civilian" program.

The newly elected Congress would like to play a role in addressing these questions, but the White House insists that the constitution empowers the executive branch alone—the president, his cabinet, and his staff—to conduct the foreign policy of the United States. The White House is wrong.

The constitution divides the conduct of foreign policy between the executive and legislative branches, depending on the issue. For example, Article I expressly empowers Congress to "regulate commerce with foreign nations"; to "define and punish" crimes committed "on the high seas" and "against the law of nations"; to declare war; and to make rules governing "land and naval forces."

Even when it comes to making treaties, the Senate must approve presidential decisions by a two-thirds vote, and it must approve the appointment of ambassadors by a majority vote.

The framers intended this division of authority as part of its insistence on checks and balances, to assure that important decisions—including those affecting foreign policy—had to achieve the support of both the executive and legislative branches.

Its purpose was not to assure gridlock, but neither was it to allow one branch alone to make all important foreign policy decisions. Its purpose was to try to achieve a modicum of agreement, through negotiation and compromise, between the branches.

How does this constitutional division of power impact the current negotiations with Iran over its nuclear program, especially in light of the current partisan division between a Democratic president and a Republican-controlled Senate and House?

The answer depends on whether Congress chooses to assert its constitutional power to participate in foreign policy decisions.

It is arguable that any deal with Iran will be enough like a treaty to warrant Senate approval, but even if that were not the case, any deal would necessarily require the removal of sanctions enacted by Congress. And Congress plainly has the power to refuse to reduce sanctions and indeed to strengthen them.

So President Obama will not have a completely free hand in making a deal with Iran. Nor should he. A president's term is fixed by the constitution, and there is a danger that a president may be somewhat shortsighted in his view of foreign policy and willing to kick the can down the road in order to preserve his legacy. Congress, on the other hand, is a continuing institution with overlapping terms and significant responsibility in assuring that the short-term interests of any given administration do not endanger the long-term interests of the country. That is why Congress should demand a role in the ongoing negotiations with Iran.

The president may, however, insist that he and he alone has the authority to make a deal with Iran. This may create a constitutional conflict between the popular branches that may have to be resolved by the third branch of our government, namely judges appointed for life. It is unclear how the Supreme Court would resolve such a conflict. Indeed a case currently pending before the justices poses the issue of which branch gets to make foreign policy decisions in the context of a dispute between the executive and the legislature over whether Jerusalem is part of Israel for purposes of the passport of an American child born in Jerusalem. Although this issue is both narrow and highly technical and involves passports, which are administered by the executive branch, the High Court may render a decision using broad language that implicates the Iranian negotiations. So we have to wait and see what the Supreme Court does and says. In the meantime Congress should not abdicate its responsibility to advise the president on this important foreign policy issue.

≈

PART V.
CLOSING THE DEAL

IN THE BEGINNING OF 2015, *it was becoming clear that a deal would be struck, and it looked like it would allow Iran to become a nuclear weapons power within a relatively short time frame—around a decade. This reality set off alarm bells in Israel, Saudi Arabia, and other Sunni Arab capitals. It also set off alarm bells among many Americans—Democrats, Republicans, and Independents—concerned for their own safety as well as their allies.*

On 21 January 2015, it was announced that Israeli Prime Minister Benjamin Netanyahu had been invited by the Speaker of the House— Republican John Boehner—to address a joint session of Congress, and that Netanyahu had accepted the invitation. This set off a firestorm of criticism that focused on two issues: first, the invitation had been extended by the Republican Speaker, and was thus seen as partisan in the American political context; second, it was extended only to Israel's conservative prime minister and not to his liberal opponent, Isaac Herzog, who was running against him in the Israeli election that was then under way. That decision was seen as partisan in the Israeli political context.

Some Democratic members of Congress immediately announced that they would boycott Netanyahu's appearance. I wrote an article in the Wall Street Journal condemning such a boycott. I also spoke to some key members of the Senate and House in an effort to persuade them that regardless of their views on the wisdom of the decision to invite Netanyahu, they should not boycott his speech. I helped to change the mind of Congressman Charles Rangel, the head of the Black Caucus, who had originally announced that he would participate in the boycott. I told him that if he, along with other members of the Black Caucus, boycotted the prime minister of the nation-state of the Jewish people, their action would be perceived—fairly or unfairly—as a breach in the traditional Black-Jewish alliance. He seemed to resonate to that argument and others that I offered, and he changed his mind and came to the Netanyahu speech.[112]

I was invited to attend the speech and sit next to the prime minister's wife, Sara, and Eli and Marion Wiesel, which I did.

The articles that follow were written during the run up to the deal and immediately following its signing.

A. *Democrats Should Not Boycott Netanyahu*[113]

As a liberal Democrat who twice campaigned for President Barack Obama, I am appalled that some Democratic members of Congress are planning to boycott the speech of Israeli Prime Minister Benjamin Netanyahu on 3 March to a joint session of Congress. At bottom, this controversy is not mainly about protocol and politics—it is about the constitutional system of checks and balances and the separation of powers.

Under the Constitution, the executive and legislative branches share responsibility for making and implementing important foreign policy decisions. Congress has a critical role to play in scrutinizing the decisions of the president when these decisions involve national security, relationships with allies, and the threat of nuclear proliferation.

Congress has every right to invite, even over the president's strong objection, any world leader or international expert who can assist its members in formulating appropriate responses to the current deal being considered with Iran regarding its nuclear weapons program. Indeed, it is the responsibility of every member of Congress to listen to Prime Minister Netanyahu, who probably knows more about this issue than any world leader, because it threatens the very existence of the nation-state of the Jewish people.

Congress has the right to disagree with the prime minister, but the idea that some members of Congress will not give him the courtesy of listening violates protocol and basic decency to a far greater extent than anything Mr. Netanyahu is accused of doing for having accepted an invitation from Congress.

Recall that President Obama sent British Prime Minister David Cameron to lobby Congress with phone calls last month against conditionally imposing new sanctions on Iran if the deal were to fail. What the president objects to is not that Mr. Netanyahu will speak to Congress, but the content of what he intends to say. This constitutes a direct intrusion on the power of Congress and on the constitutional separation of powers.

Not only should all members of Congress attend Mr. Netanyahu's speech, but President Obama—as a constitutional scholar—should urge members of Congress to do their constitutional duty of listening to opposing views in order to check and balance the policies of the administration.

Whether one agrees or disagrees with Speaker John Boehner's decision to invite Mr. Netanyahu or Mr. Netanyahu's decision to accept, no legal scholar can dispute that Congress has the power to act independently of the president in matters of foreign policy. Whether any deal with Iran would technically constitute a treaty requiring Senate confirmation, it is certainly treaty-like in its impact. Moreover, the president can't implement the deal without some action or inaction by Congress.

Congress also has a role in implementing the president's promise—made on behalf of our nation as a whole—that Iran will never be allowed to develop nuclear weapons. That promise seems to be in the process of being broken, as reports in the media and Congress circulate that the deal on the table contains a sunset provision that would allow Iran to develop nuclear weapons after a certain number of years.

Once it became clear that Iran will eventually be permitted to become a nuclear weapon power, it has already become such a power for practical purposes. The Saudis and the Arab Emirates will not wait until Iran turns the last screw on its nuclear bomb. As soon as this deal is struck, with its sunset provision, these countries would begin to develop their own nuclear weapon programs, as would other countries in the region. If Congress thinks this is a bad deal, it has the responsibility to act.

Another reason members of Congress should not boycott Mr. Netanyahu's speech is that support for Israel has always been a bipartisan issue. The decision by some members to boycott Israel's prime minister endangers this bipartisan support. This will not only hurt Israel but will also endanger support for Democrats among pro-Israel voters. I certainly would never vote for or support a member of Congress who walked out on Israel's prime minister.

One should walk out on tyrants, bigots, and radical extremists, as the United States did when Iran's Mahmoud Ahmadinejad denied the Holocaust and called for Israel's destruction at the United Nations. To use such an extreme tactic against our closest ally, and the Middle East's only vibrant democracy, is not only to insult Israel's prime minister but to put Israel in a category in which it does not belong.

So let members of Congress who disagree with the prime minister's decision to accept Speaker Boehner's invitation express that disagreement privately and even publicly, but let them not walk out on a speech from which they may learn a great deal and which may help them prevent the president from making a disastrous foreign policy mistake. Inviting a prime minister of an ally to educate Congress about a pressing foreign policy decision is in the highest tradition of our democratic system of separation of powers and checks and balances.

B. *The White House Must Respond to Netanyahu's Important New Proposal*[114]

I was in the House gallery when Israel's prime minister, Benjamin Netanyahu, delivered a logical and compelling critique of the deal now on the table regarding Iran's ambitions to obtain nuclear weapons. He laid out a new fact-based proposal that has shifted the burden of persuasion to the White House.

His new proposal is that "If the world powers are not prepared to insist that Iran change its behavior *before* a deal is signed, at the very least they should insist that Iran change its behavior before a deal *expires*." His argument is that without such a precondition, the ten-year sunset provision paves, rather than blocks, the way to an Iranian nuclear arsenal, even if Iran were to continue to export terrorism, to bully nations in the region, and to call for the extermination of Israel.

With logic that seems unassailable, Netanyahu has said that the alternative to this bad deal is not war, but rather "a better deal that Israel and its neighbors might not like, but which we could live with, literally." Netanyahu then outlined his condition for a better deal: namely that before the sun is allowed to set on prohibiting Iran from developing nuclear weapons, the mullahs must first meet three conditions: stop exporting terrorism, stop intruding in the affairs of other countries, and stop threatening the existence of Israel.

If the mullahs reject these three reasonable conditions, it will demonstrate that they have no real interest in joining the international community and abiding by its rules. If they accept these conditions, then the sunset provision will not kick in automatically but will require that Iran demonstrate a willingness to play by the rules, before the rules allow it to develop nuclear weapons.

Instead of attacking the messenger, as the White House has done, the administration now has an obligation to engage with Netanyahu in the marketplace of ideas, rather than in a cacophony of name-calling, and to respond to Netanyahu's argument *on its merit*. There may be persuasive responses, but we have not yet heard them.

The decision to accept or reject a deal with Iran over its nuclear weapons program may be the most important foreign policy issue of the twenty-first century. Many members of Congress, perhaps most, agree with the prime minister of Israel rather than with the president of the United States on this issue. Under our system of separation of powers, Congress is a fully coequal branch of the government, and no major decision of the kind involved in this deal should be made over its opposition. Perhaps the president can persuade Congress to support this deal, but he must engage with, rather than ignore, our duly elected representatives of the people.

The administration and its supporters, particularly those who boycotted the prime minister's speech, focus on the so-called lack of protocol by which Netanyahu was invited by the Speaker of the House. Imagine, however, the same protocol for a speaker who *favored* rather than *opposed* the current deal. The White

House and its supporters would be welcoming a prime minister who supported the president's deal, as they did British Prime Minister David Cameron when he was sent in to lobby the Senate in favor of the administration's position. So the protocol issue is largely a pretext. The administration is upset more by the *content* of Netanyahu's speech than by the manner in which he received the invitation.

This is too important an issue to get sidetracked by the formalities of protocol. The speech has now been given. It was a balanced speech that included praise for the president, for the Democrats, for Congress, and for the American people. Prime Minister Netanyahu was at his diplomatic best. In my view, he was also at his substantive best in laying out the case against the administration's negotiating position with regard to Iran, especially the unconditional sunset provision.

The administration must now answer one fundamental question: Why would you allow the Iranian regime to develop nuclear weapons in ten years, if at that time they were still exporting terrorism, bullying their Arab neighbors, and threatening to exterminate Israel? Why not, at the very least, condition any "sunset" provision on a change in the actions of this criminal regime? The answer may be that we can't get them to agree to this condition. If that is the case, then this is indeed a bad deal that is worse than no deal. It would be far better to increase economic sanctions and other pressures, rather than to end them in exchange for a mere postponement of Iran obtaining a nuclear arsenal.

There may be better answers, but the ball is now in Obama's court to provide them, rather than to avoid answering Netanyahu's reasonable questions by irrelevant answers about "protocol" and personal attacks on the messenger. Israel deserves better. The world deserves better. The American people deserve better. And Congress deserves better.

An unconditional sunset provision is an invitation to an Iran that continues to export terrorism, bully neighbors, and threaten Israel—but with a nuclear arsenal to terrorize the entire world. This would be "a game changer," to quote President Obama's words from several years ago, when he promised that he would *never* allow Iran to develop nuclear weapons. Suddenly, "never" has become "soon." Congress should insist that any provision allowing Iran to develop nuclear weapons after ten years must at the very least be conditioned on a significant change of behavior by the world's most dangerous regime.

c. *Supporters of the Deal Are Strengthening Iran's Negotiating Position*[115]

Despite repeating the mantra that "no deal is better than a bad deal" with Iran, the United States seems to be negotiating on the basis of a belief that the worst possible outcome of the current negotiations is no deal. Many supporters of the deal that is now apparently on the table are arguing that there is no realistic alternative to this deal. That sort of thinking out loud empowers the Iranian negotiators to demand more and compromise less, because they believe—and have been told by American supporters of the deal—that the United States has no alternative but to agree to a deal that is acceptable to the Iranians.

A perfect example of this mindset was Fareed Zakaria on his CNN show this past Sunday. He had a loaded panel of two experts and a journalist favoring the deal, and one journalist opposed. This followed Zakaria's opening essay in favor of the deal. All those in favor made the same point: that this deal is better than no deal, and that any new proposal—for example, to condition the sunset provision on Iran stopping the export of terrorism and threatening to destroy Israel—is likely to be rejected by Iran, and is therefore, by definition, "irrational" or "unproductive" because it would result in no deal.

The upshot of this position is that Iran essentially gets a veto over any proposal, but the United States does not get to make new proposals. If it were true that this deal is better than no deal, it would follow that any proposed change in this deal that Iran doesn't like is a nonstarter.

That's why Netanyahu's reasonable proposal that the sunset provision be conditioned on changes in Iranian actions and words has been pooh-poohed by the so-called "experts." They haven't tried to respond on the merits. Instead, they are satisfied to argue that Iran would never accept such conditions, and therefore the proposal should be rejected as a deal breaker.

This is the worst sort of negotiation strategy imaginable: telling the other side that any proposal that is not acceptable to them will be taken off the table, and that any leader who offers it will be attacked as a deal breaker. This approach—attacking Netanyahu without responding to his proposal on its merits—characterizes the approach of the administration and its supporters.

We will now never know whether Iran *might have* accepted a conditional sunset provision, because the advocates of the current deal, both inside and outside the administration, have told Iran that if they reject this proposal, it will be withdrawn because it endangers the deal. What incentive would the Iranians then have to consider this proposal on its merits? None!

The current mindset of the deal's advocates is that the United States needs the deal more than the Iranians do. That is why the US is constantly leaking reports that the mullahs may be reluctant to sign even this one-sided deal, which has shifted perceptibly in favor of the Iranian position over the past several months. But the truth is that Iran, which is suffering greatly from the combination of sanctions and dropping oil prices, needs this deal—a deal that would end sanctions and allow it unconditionally to develop nuclear weapons within ten years. That doesn't necessarily mean they will accept it. They may push for even more compromises on the part of the United States. The reality is that we are in a far stronger negotiating position than advocates of the deal have asserted, but we are negotiating from weakness because we have persuaded the Iranians that we need the deal—any deal—more than they do.

Most Israelis seem to be against the current deal, especially the unconditional sunset provision. Author David Grossman, a left-wing dove who is almost always critical of Netanyahu, has accused the United States of "criminal naiveté." He opposes Netanyahu's reelection but urges the world to listen to what Netanyahu told Congress.

> But what [Netanyahu] says about Iran and the destructive part it is playing in the Middle East cannot and should not be ignored," Grossman said. "Netanyahu is right when he says that according to the emerging deal there is nothing to prevent the Iranians from developing a nuclear bomb once the deal expires in another 10 years, and on this matter there is no difference in Israel between Left and Right.

There are considerable differences, however, between the Obama administration's negotiating position and the views of most Israelis, Saudis, Emiratis, Egyptians, and Jordanians—as well as most members of our own Congress. We can get a better deal, but supporters of a deal must abandon their unhelpful public claims that the current deal is the best we can get.

D. *President Is Not Commander in Chief of Foreign Policy*[116]

Politicians should stop referring to the president of the United States as "the commander in chief," as he is often referred to. Most recently, Hillary Clinton, whom I admire, said the following about Republican senators who wrote an open letter to Iran:

"Either these senators were trying to be helpful to the Iranians or harmful to the Commander-in-Chief in the midst of high-stakes international diplomacy."

But the president is not the commander in chief for purposes of diplomatic negotiations. This characterization mistakenly implies that President Obama—or any president—is *our* commander, and that his decisions should receive special deference. This is a misreading of our constitution, which creates a presidency that is subject to the checks and balances of coequal branches of the government. The president is *only* the commander in chief of "the Army and Navy of the United States, and of the militia of the several states, when called into the actual service of the United States." This provision was intended to assure civilian control over the military and to serve as a check on military power.

The only people he is empowered to command are soldiers, sailors, and members of the militia—not ordinary citizens.

This important limitation on the president's power is highly relevant to the current debate about Congress having the authority to check the president's decision to make the deal that is currently being negotiated with Iran. The Constitution is clear about this. The President is not the commander in chief of our nation's foreign policy. When he is involved in "high-stakes international diplomacy," his involvement is not as commander in chief of our armed forces, but rather as negotiator in chief, whose negotiations are subject to the checks and balances of the other branches.

As president, he cannot even declare war, though he can decide how a war should be fought after Congress declares it. He cannot make a treaty without the approval of two-thirds of the Senate. He cannot appoint ambassadors without the consent of the Senate. And he cannot terminate sanctions that were imposed by Congress without Congress changing the law. Were he the commander in chief of our country—as Putin is of Russia or as Ali Khamenei is of Iran—he could simply command that all of these things be done. But our Constitution separates the powers of government—the power to command—into three coequal branches. The armed forces are different: power is vested in one commander in chief.

To be sure, when politicians call our president the commander in chief, they are using that term rhetorically. But it is a dangerous rhetoric, because it suggests a concentration, rather than a division, of power. Military metaphors are as inappropriate in a democracy as is martial law, which does empower the executive to act as the commander of all people, but only in cases of extreme emergency.

So let's describe the president by his actual constitutional role: the head of the executive branch of our tripod government that stands on three equal legs. As the head of the executive branch, he gets to *negotiate* treaties, agreements, and other bilateral and multilateral deals. But Congress has a say in whether to *approve* what the president has negotiated.

Turning to the deal with Iran over nuclear weapons, there are sharp disagreements between the executive branch and the legislative branch over the merits of what appears to be the deal now on the table. No agreement has yet been reached, but assume, for argument's sake, that the president negotiates a deal with which a majority of Congress fundamentally disagrees. Who gets the final word? That depends on several factors.

First, of course, is whether the deal negotiated by the president constitutes a "treaty" within the meaning of the constitution. If it does, then it requires the formal ratification of the Senate. The Obama administration has taken the position that this is merely an executive agreement and not a treaty. That, of course, is a knife that cuts both ways, because treaties are binding until formally revoked, whereas executive agreements can be undone by future presidents. The law is anything but clear as to what makes a bilateral or multilateral agreement a treaty, but this one has elements that are treaty-like in its content. So even if it does not formally meet the definition of a treaty, this agreement should require some form of approval by the legislative branch, particularly if it is to remain an enduring part of American foreign policy.

Another factor that impacts the role of Congress is whether the agreement requires Congress to remove existing sanctions that were put in place by congressional action. If it does, then the approval of Congress for the removal of such sanctions will be required. This deal would seem therefore to require congressional approval, since it includes the removal of congressional sanctions. The president, however, does have some sanctioning power, and he can remove sanctions that he or past presidents have imposed.

These important issues will be debated over the next weeks and months, but what should not be debated is the role of the president in a democracy based on the separation of powers. So let's stop calling the head of our executive branch the commander in chief, and let's stop creating the false impression that the president alone can make an enforceable and enduring deal with Iran regarding its nuclear weapons program.

I have been a strident critic of President Obama's policy toward Iran, especially how he and his team have been negotiating with that belligerent regime over its nuclear weapons program. But opposition to one aspect of the Obama policies should not be mistaken for opposition to President Obama himself or to the many achievements of his administration, particularly in the domestic area.

Having just listened to his speech at a conservative Jewish congregation in Washington, I was reminded why I supported him both times he ran for president, as well as when he ran for the US Senate. Barack Obama is a good and decent person who admires the Jewish people and supports Israel's right to exist as the nation-state of the Jewish people as well as its right to defend itself against attacks, both domestic and foreign. He disagrees with the Netanyahu administration on several issues.

On some of these issues, such as settlement building, I tend to agree with Obama. On other issues, such as the Iran negotiations, I tend to agree with Prime Minister Netanyahu.

On a personal level, I do not think that President Obama has handled his relationship with Prime Minister Netanyahu in a mature and productive fashion.

Having been provoked by Speaker John Boehner's invitation to have Netanyahu speak to Congress, President Obama acted in a petulant manner that exacerbated the differences between them. I also disapprove of how President Obama handled Netanyahu's statements regarding the two-state solution. Recall that on the evening of Netanyahu's reelection in March, he made a statement suggesting that the time was not ripe for the establishment of a Palestinian state. Immediately following his election, Netanyahu reasserted his commitment to the two-state solution. Instead of reacting in a statesmanlike way by focusing on Netanyahu's positive restatement, Obama reemphasized his opposition to Netanyahu's previous negative statements. This was poor politics, poor statesmanship, and poor psychology.

Regarding the deal with Iran, President Obama had said that between accepting the deal and rejecting it, the only realistic option is to accept it. He may be right, but he was wrong to get us into the position where the only options may be bad and worse.

I will continue to be critical of Obama and his administration where I believe criticism is warranted, but I will continue to express approval and admiration for the president when he acts in a positive fashion.

President Obama's speech to the Jewish congregation in Washington was excellent. He talked about shared values between the US and Israel and between him and the Jewish community. His policies with regard to health care and many other domestic issues are consistent with those of a majority of American Jews. We should neither demonize nor lionize our president. We should criticize him where criticism is warranted, praise him where praise is justified, and encourage him to be supportive of Israel. There is too much extremism at play when it comes to President Obama. People who hate him, hate him too much and without justification.

Some people who love him, love him too much and without nuanced criticism.

So let's continue to watch carefully how this administration deals with foreign policy issues, especially with regard to Israel and Iran, and let's be constructive and nuanced in both our criticism and our support.

In his speech to the congregation, President Obama invited "scrutiny" of his foreign policy actions, particularly with regard to Iran. We should accept his invitation and offer good faith and constructive criticism.

F. *Does This Deal Prevent Iran from Developing a*
    Nuclear Weapon?[118]

Does the proposed deal with Iran actually prevent the mullahs from ever developing a nuclear weapon? Or does it merely delay them for a period of years? That is the key question that has not yet been clearly answered.

In his statement on the deal, US President Barack Obama seemed to suggest that Iran will never be allowed to develop a nuclear weapon. He said that this "long-term deal with Iran… will prevent it from obtaining a nuclear weapon." He then repeated this assurance: "because of this deal, the international community will be able to verify that the Islamic Republic of Iran will not be able to develop a nuclear weapon." These seemingly categorical statements were intended to assure the world that Obama would keep his earlier promise that Iran will never be allowed to develop nuclear weapons.

But is that what the deal itself does? Or, as stated by its critics, does it actually assure that Iran will be allowed to develop a nuclear arsenal after a short delay of several years? That is the key question that the Obama administration has refused to answer directly. It must do so before Congress can be asked to buy a pig in a poke for the American people.

There is an enormous difference between a deal that merely delays Iran's development of a nuclear arsenal for a period of years and a deal that prevents Iran from ever developing a nuclear arsenal. Prime Minister Benjamin Netanyahu and many other critics of this deal describe it as merely a delay, while the Obama administration seems to be suggesting by its rhetoric that the deal will prevent Iran from ever obtaining a nuclear weapon.

The devil is not so much in the details as in the broad outlines of this deal and its understanding by the parties. Does it or does it not allow Iran to develop nuclear weapons after a relatively short moratorium? Iran certainly seems to believe that it does, Israel certainly believes that it does, and many in Congress— both Republicans and Democrats—seem to believe that it does. But the president seems to be telling the American public and the world that these critics are wrong: that Iran will never be allowed to develop a nuclear weapon under this deal. Yet, just a few months ago, he seemed more cautious and candid in discussing his "fear" that "in year 13, 14, 15, they have advanced centrifuges that enrich uranium fairly rapidly, and at that point the breakout times would have shrunk almost down to zero."[119] He also said that we have had assurances of a yearlong breakout time "for at least well over a decade," implying that after that indeterminate time frame, the assurances will no longer be in place. Obama's statement, despite its confusing and ambiguous context, has raised deep concerns among critics of the deal. Moreover, the text of the deal includes time frames of 8½ years, 10 years, and 15 years, which also generates confusion at a time when clarity is essential.

So which is it? Congress has a right to know, and so do the American people. Is it a postponement for an uncertain number of years—8½ years, 10, 13, 14, 15—of Iran's ability to develop a nuclear weapon? Or is it an assurance that "Iran will not be able to develop a nuclear weapon?"

The Obama administration insists that this is not a "treaty," but rather a "deal." A deal is a contract, and for a contract to be valid, there must be a "meeting of the minds." But has there been a meeting of the minds over the central issue of whether this deal allows Iran to develop a nuclear weapon after a moratorium whose precise time frame is unclear? And if there has been a meeting of the minds over this issue, what exactly is it?

Certainly the words of the Iranians are not the same as the words of Obama. Whose words accurately represent the meaning of the contract we are being asked to sign?

The time has now come to be crystal clear about the meaning of this deal. If it is intended to prevent Iran from ever developing nuclear weapons, the president must say so in the clearest of terms, and he must get the Iranians to express agreement with that interpretation. Ambiguity may be a virtue at the beginning of a negotiation, but it is a vice in interpreting and implementing a deal with such high stakes.

Recall that former US president Bill Clinton made similar assurances with regard to North Korea back in 1994—as the accompanying chart shows. But within a few short years of signing a deal that he assured us would require the dismantling of North Korea's nuclear program, that country tested its first nuclear weapon. It now has a nuclear arsenal. How can we be sure that Iran will not act in a similar fashion?

The deal with Iran has been aptly characterized as a "leap of faith," "a bet," and a "roll of the dice" by David Sanger in a news analysis for the *New York Times*. The gamble is that by the time the most restrictive provisions of the deal expire, Iran will be a different country with more reasonable leaders. But can the world, and especially the nations most at risk from an Iranian nuclear arsenal, depend on faith, bets, and dice when they know that the last time the nuclear dice were rolled, they came up snake eyes for America and its allies when North Korea ended up with nuclear weapons.

The burden of persuasion is now on the Obama administration to demonstrate that Obama was accurately describing the deal when he said that it will "prevent" Iran from "obtaining a nuclear weapon." It is a heavy burden that will be—and should be—difficult to satisfy.

President Obama's Statement on the Nuclear Agreement with Iran (14 July 2015)*	President Clinton's Remarks on the Nuclear Agreement with North Korea (18 October 1994)†

On the Objectives of the Agreements

"After two years of negotiations, the United States, together with our international partners, has achieved something that decades of animosity has not: a comprehensive long-term deal with Iran that will prevent it from obtaining a nuclear weapon. This deal demonstrates that American diplomacy can bring about real and meaningful change, change that makes our country and the world safer and more secure."	"Today, after 16 months of intense and difficult negotiations with North Korea, we have completed an agreement that will make the United States, the Korean Peninsula, and the world safer."

On the Content and Implementation of the Agreements

"Every pathway to a nuclear weapon is cut off, and the inspection and transparency regime necessary to verify that objective will be put in place…. Because of this deal we will for the first time be in a position to verify all of these commitments. That means this deal is not built on trust. It is built on verification."	"This agreement represents the first step on the road to a nuclear-free Korean Peninsula. It does not rely on trust. Compliance will be certified by the International Atomic Energy Agency."

On the Implications of the Agreements

"A different path, one of tolerance and peaceful resolution of conflict, leads to more integration into the global economy, more engagement with the international community and the ability of the Iranian people to prosper and thrive. This deal offers an opportunity to move in a new direction. We should seize it."	"It's [this agreement] a crucial step toward drawing North Korea into the global community…. The United States and North Korea have also agreed to ease trade restrictions and to move toward establishing liaison offices in each other's capitals. The offices will ease North Korea's isolation."

On Support for Regional Allies

"We will continue our unprecedented efforts to strengthen Israel's security, efforts that go beyond what any American administration has done before."	"And the United States has an unshakeable commitment to protect our ally and our fellow democracy South Korea. Thirty-eight thousand troops stationed on the peninsula are the guarantors of that commitment."

* "Statement by the President on Iran," White House Office of the Press Secretary, 14 July 2015

† "Remarks on the Nuclear Agreement with North Korea," William J. Clinton, 18 October 1994

G. *US Gave Away Better Options on Iran*[122]

The most compelling argument the Obama administration is offering to boost what it acknowledges is a compromise nuclear deal with Iran is this: it's better than the alternatives. That sort of pragmatic point is appealing to members of Congress, particularly skeptical Democrats who are searching for ways to support their president and who are accustomed to voting for the lesser of evils in a real-politick world where the options are often bad, worse, even worse, and worst of all.

But the question remains: How did we get ourselves into the situation where there are no good options?

We did so by beginning the negotiations with three important concessions. First, we took the military option off the table by publicly declaring that we were not militarily capable of permanently ending Iran's nuclear weapons program. Second, we took the current tough sanction regimen off the table by acknowledging that if we did not accept a deal, many of our most important partners would begin to reduce or even eliminate sanctions. Third, and most important, we took off the table the option of rejecting the deal by publicly acknowledging that if we do so, we will be worse off than if we accept even a questionable deal. Yes, the president said he would not accept a "bad" deal, but by repeatedly watering down the definition of a bad deal, and by repeatedly stating that the alternative to a deal would be disastrous, he led the Iranians to conclude we needed the deal more than they did.

These three concessions left our negotiators with little leverage and provided their Iranian counterparts with every incentive to demand more compromises from us. The result is that we pinned ourselves into a corner. As Danielle Pletka of the American Enterprise Institute put it: "The deal itself became more important than what was in it." President Obama seems to have confirmed that assessment when he said: "Put simply, no deal means a greater chance of more war in the Middle East."

Only time will tell whether this deal decreases or increases the likelihood of more war. But one thing is clear: by conveying those stark alternatives to Iranian negotiators, we weakened our bargaining position.

The reality is that there were always alternatives, though they became less realistic as the negotiations progressed. We could have stuck to the original red lines—nonnegotiable demands— from the beginning. These included on-the-spot inspections of all facilities rather than the nearly month-long notice that will allow the Iranians to hide what they are doing; shutting down all facilities specifically designed for nuclear weapons production; maintaining the embargo on missiles and other sophisticated weapons rather than allowing it to gradually be lifted; and most crucially, a written assurance that the international community will never allow Iran to develop a nuclear arsenal. The current assortment of indeterminate and varying time lines agreed to will allow Iranians to believe—and proclaim—they will soon be free of any constraints on their nuclear adventurism.

Instead, we caved early and often because the Iranians knew we desperately need a deal to implement President Obama's world vision and to enhance his legacy.

This approach to the deal—surrendering leverage from the outset—violated the most basic principles of negotiation 101. We were playing checkers against the people who invented chess, and their ayatollah checkmated our president.

But the real losers were those countries—our allies—who were not even allowed to participate in the negotiations. Virtually every Middle Eastern leader, with the exception of Syria's Assad, opposes this deal. Nor do they feel bound by it, since they did not have a vote. The deal was imposed on them, in much the same way the Chamberlain-Hitler deal was imposed on Czechoslovakia in 1938. The difference is that Czechoslovakia did not have the means to defend itself, whereas Israel and some of its Sunni neighbors do have the capacity to try to prevent Iran from developing a nuclear arsenal—which the mullahs would use to increase their hegemony over the area and to threaten Israel's security through its surrogates, Hezbollah and Hamas. Those groups would become even more aggressive under the protection of an Iranian nuclear umbrella.

The end result of this porous agreement may well be, to turn President Obama's words against his own conclusion, "a greater chance of more war in the Middle East."

Churchill correctly predicted that the Chamberlain deal with Hitler would bring war. Let's hope the Iran deal—based on deeply flawed negotiations—will not produce a similar catastrophe.

CONCLUSION

What does the future hold? Will Iran obtain a nuclear arsenal? If so, when? Will it become a "game changer?" If so, how will things change?

"Predicting is hazardous, especially about the future," says a quote attributed to various wise men. But prediction is essential to policy choices, despite the hazards of making a mistake. Some predictive mistakes, however, are more costly than others.

President Obama is staking this deal on a series of predictions—"bets," "rolls of the dice," and "faith"—that include the following:

1. Under the deal, Iran is less likely than without a deal to develop a nuclear arsenal in the short, medium, and long term;*

---

* Following the announcement of the agreed framework in April 2015, President Obama said: "My goal when I first came into office was to make sure that Iran did not get a nuclear weapon and thereby trigger a nuclear arms race in the most volatile part of the world... We're now in a position where Iran has agreed to unprecedented inspections and verifications of its program, providing assurances that it is peaceful in nature. You have them rolling back a number of pathways that they currently have available to break out and get a nuclear weapon. You have assurances that their stockpile of highly enriched uranium remains in a place where they cannot create a nuclear weapon." "Transcript: President Obama's Full NPR Interview on Iran Nuclear Deal," National Public Radio, 7 April 2015.

2. Under the deal, the Iranian regime is more likely to become part of the community of nations and to change its status from an outlaw nation that tyrannizes its own people, exports terrorism, hegemonizes its Arab neighbors, and threatens to annihilate Israel;*

3. War in the Middle East is less likely under the deal than without it.†

There are other unintended consequences that, though unpredictable, may flow directly or indirectly from the deal. They include the following:

1. New alliances may form in the Middle East. It was predicted that Saudi Arabia may have to become closer to Israel because of their common enemy. But the

---

* President Obama remarked: "What a deal would do… is take a big piece of business off the table and perhaps begin a long process in which the relationship not just between Iran and us but the relationship between Iran and the world, and the region, begins to change…. I think Iran would love to see the sanctions end immediately, and then to still have some avenues that might not be completely closed, and we can't do that." Brian Knowles, "Obama Acknowledges Broad Gaps Between 2 Sides in Iran Nuclear Talk," *New York Times*, 23 November 2014.

† In an interview with Thomas Friedman, shortly after announcing the agreement, President Obama said: "This deal… by a wide margin is the most definitive path by which Iran will not get a nuclear weapon, and we will be able to achieve that with the full cooperation of the world community and without having to engage in another war in the Middle East." Thomas Friedman, "Obama Makes His Case on Iran Nuclear Deal," *New York Times*, 14 July 2015.

opposite may result as well: seeing the handwriting on the wall, and sensing the growing strength of Iran and the shrinking influence of the US, Saudi Arabia may begin to hedge its bets by moving closer to Iran. To demonstrate how unpredictable the Middle East is, within days of the deal being signed, the King of Saudi Arabia met with the leaders of Hamas, a virulently anti-Israel terrorist organization that is both an offshoot of the Muslim Brotherhood and a client of Iran[123]—both of which the Saudis have long regarded as mortal enemies. But in the Middle East, power attracts, and this deal empowers Iran as never before.

2. Iran, with hundreds of billions more dollars in its treasury, may increase its funding of terrorism by surrogate groups such as Hezbollah and others in various parts of the Middle East. On the other hand, as a regional superpower, it may have a growing interest in stability and in defeating other terrorist groups, particularly ISIS (or ISIL) and Al Qaeda.

3. Despite its insistence that this deal does not reduce its enmity toward the US,[124] it is possible that it may, over time, empower those within the Iranian regime who are less hostile to America, especially following the demise of Ayatollah Ali Khamenei. This deal is—and is seen in Iran as—a major victory for the Islamic Republic, and the victory was brought about largely by "moderates"—a relative term when it comes to Iran—over the objection of some of the most hard-line elements in the regime. Although the Iranian leadership regards the

US as having shown weakness in its negotiation, and although it regards the threat of any military action by the US as having been dissipated, it still understands that America has the most powerful military in the world, that Obama will not be president for long, and that the outcome of the 2016 election is unpredictable. So even if the Iranian regime makes decisions based on power rather than principle, the enduring military and economic power wielded by the US and its allies creates a disincentive toward escalating the conflict—at least until Iran becomes a nuclear weapons power.

4. This brings us to the most unpredictable consequence of the deal: If and when Iran breaks out and develops a nuclear arsenal—and that may happen in a decade even if the Iranian leadership complies with the deal in full—how will it deploy its newfound power? President Obama has told us that an Iran with nuclear weapons would be a "game changer" that would be dangerous to our national security interests and those of our allies. Is there any reason to believe that it will be less of a game changer in ten years than it would be now? That is certainly what the president—and indeed the rest of the world—hopes will happen, but we cannot predict such a positive outcome with any degree of confidence, because although ten years is a blink of an eye for purposes of assessing dangers to national security, it is an eternity for purposes of making predictions. That is why this deal is indeed a roll of the dice—or perhaps more aptly a game of Russian roulette for us and our allies. Although the odds of losing in Russian roulette are only

one in six, no one would praise a leader who got us
into a situation where playing Russian roulette is the
best alternative available, especially if we got into that
situation by putting our own weapons away.

Having concluded that the negotiations with Iran were deeply
flawed and that the resulting deal is extremely dangerous, it might
be expected that I would advocate its rejection by Congress by
means of overriding the promised presidential veto. But the latter
conclusion doesn't necessarily follow from the former. Perhaps
one of the worst consequences of the negotiation and deal is that
they put us in a position where *rejecting* a bad deal may be worse
than accepting it. It is impossible to know.

If the deal were to be rejected by Congress, and accepted by
Iran, most of the sanctions—those imposed by the Security
Council, by our Western European partners, by China and
Russia, and even those imposed by the president without congressional approval—would quickly disappear. The crippling
sanctions regime would end, and Iran would get much of the
hundreds of billions of dollars of sanction relief it has been
seeking. Secretary of State John Kerry acknowledged this in an
interview on 19 July 2015 on *Face the Nation*:

> If Congress says no to this deal, then there will be no
> restraints on Iran. There will be no sanctions left. Our
> friends in this effort will desert us.

Moreover, the military option would remain off the table,
because it can be deployed only by the president, not by
Congress, and President Obama is now not likely to use military
force to prevent Iran from developing nuclear weapons. When
Secretary Kerry said "there will be no constraints on Iran" if

Congress rejects the deal, he was telling us and Iran that no military constraints would be imposed, despite statements that all options remain on the table. That is certainly the way the Iranian leaders see it, as evidenced by Ayatollah Ali Khomeini's statement on 6 May 2015, that "The Iranian nation does not tolerate negotiation under the shadow of threat" and that the US cannot "do a damn thing."[125] Israeli officials view Kerry's statement as "thinly veiled efforts to muzzle criticism" of the deal.[126] My proposal, made in September 2013 and echoed recently by Thomas Friedman, is that Congress should now authorize the president "to use force to prevent Iran from ever becoming a nuclear weapons state." But such a law would merely authorize, not compel, the president "to destroy—without warning or negotiation—any attempt by Tehran to build an atomic bomb."[127] It would be a good step to take, whether or not the presidential veto of a vote disapproving of the deal were upheld.

The result of a congressional rejection of the deal could be a win-win for the Iranian regime, because they would have accomplished their three goals—ending most of the sanctions, taking the military option off the table, and presenting themselves to the international community as reasonable leaders who were willing to sign the deal. But if Congress were to reject the deal, the Iranians would not feel bound to honor its provisions regarding centrifuges, inspections, and other constraints—temporary though they may be—on moving toward becoming a nuclear weapons power.* Indeed, there is a cautionary tale to be found

---

*   Under Iranian law, the Parliament must approve the deal, and it has postponed its decision until after our Congress decides, in order "to avoid losing face if the agreement is rejected in the US." Thomas Erdbrink, "Iran Lawmakers to Wait 80 Days Before Voting on Nuclear Deal," *New York Times*, 21 July 2015.

in our recent history: the failure of the Republican-controlled Congress to fully implement the terms of President Clinton's nuclear agreement with North Korea provided an excuse for that country to renege on the terms of the deal, and successfully resume its pursuit of nuclear weapons. So President Obama may well be correct when he says that the current deal is "a better outcome for America, Israel, and our Arab allies than any other alternative on the table." But even if that were true—and it is speculative at best—it is damning with faint praise if all the available outcomes are bad, and if President Obama got us into the situation when there could have been better alternatives that are now no longer on the table. This variation on Hobson's choice—call it "Obama's choice"—would not have been necessary had President Obama kept, and communicated to Iran, the promise he repeatedly made before he was reelected: namely that "we are determined to prevent Iran from acquiring nuclear weapons [so] rest assured, we will take no options off the table. We have been clear." If Iran had been persuaded that the US would never allow it to develop nuclear weapons, and that enduring the crippling sanctions was therefore foolish, it might well have accepted President Obama's original red lines. But because the Obama administration changed its policy after his reelection and the subsequent midterms—from prevention to containment and from permanent to temporary—the Iranians were able to outmaneuver us. The entirely preventable result may well be that within a decade, Iran will have a nuclear arsenal that in President Obama's own words will "pose a security threat not only to the [Middle East] but also to the United States."[128]

It is possible, of course, that Obama's "bet"—his "roll of the dice"—could produce the result we all hope for: namely a reformed Iran that does not pursue its nuclear weapons ambitions when the deal allows it to continue to spin centrifuges capable of producing nuclear weapons. If the bet pays off, and the deal encourages Iran to give up its role as a rogue-state sponsor of terrorism that threatens the stability of the Middle East and Israel's existence, and Iran rejoins the international community, then it will become a positive legacy for President Obama—perhaps his most important international accomplishment. This possibility should encourage the Obama administration in its waning months to do everything in its power to move Iran in this direction so that the hope for a good outcome is realized.

But hope is different from "faith," though neither is an appropriate basis on which to "roll the dice" on a nuclear deal that might well threaten the security of the world.

Because the stakes are so high, Congress has an especially important constitutional role to play as the primary institution empowered to serve as a check and balance on the executive branch. Under our constitution, the power to make long-term foreign policy decisions that affect the security of our nation and the world is vested jointly in the executive and legislative branches. President Obama has sought to diminish the role of Congress with regard to the Iran deal by:

1. Declaring it to be a sole executive agreement rather than a treaty or a joint executive-legislative agreement;

2. Initially opposing even the Corker Bill and then promising to veto any rejection of the deal by Congress;

3. Agreeing to submit the deal to the United Nations Security Council before Congress had the ability to consider it;

4. Trying to marginalize opponents of the deal as politically motivated partisans who are the same people who pushed us into war with Iraq, and who present "overheated and often dishonest arguments…";[129]

5. Describing the only alternatives to the deal as either Iran quickly developing nuclear weapons or America going to war with Iran,* and insisting that this deal is better than any alternatives now on the table.

In order to determine whether rejecting the deal at this point would be worse than accepting a bad deal that could have been a lot better, it is imperative that Congress perform its constitutional duty to check and balance the executive branch by asking and demanding answers to the following questions:

1. Even after the expiration of the nuclear agreement, does Article iii. of the "Preamble and General Provisions"—stating that "…under no circumstances will Iran ever seek, develop or acquire any nuclear weapons"[130]—mean that Iran would be found in breach of its commitments under this deal were it to try to develop a nuclear bomb after 10 years?† If so, what would be

---

* Some commentators have suggested that war would be far from inevitable, were the JCPOA to collapse; see Anshel Pfeffer, "Iran-Deal Evangelists are the Biggest Threat to Success," *Haaretz*, 30 July 2015

† In addition to the explicit assurances contained in the JCPOA, and given the agreement's repeated reference to the Non-Proliferation Treaty, which Iran signed in 1968, it should be assumed that Iran is bound never to develop nuclear weapons under this agreement. However, Iran has already violated the NPT repeatedly and has refused

the consequences? Will the president explicitly state that his understanding of the deal is that it precludes Iran from "ever" seeking to "develop or acquire any nuclear weapons"? Will the other P5 plus one? Will Iran?

2. After the major constraints contained in the deal end, or were the deal to collapse at any point, how long would it take Iran to produce a deliverable nuclear bomb?

3. Would the United States allow Iran to begin production of a nuclear arsenal when the major constraints of the deal end?

4. Does the deal reflect a reversal in policy from President Obama's pre-reelection promise that "my policy is not containment; my policy is to prevent them from getting a nuclear weapon"?

5. If not, will President Obama now announce that it is still the policy of the United States that Iran will not be allowed to develop a nuclear weapon? And will he sign legislation, as advocated by Thomas Friedman, myself, and others, that authorizes "this President and future presidents to use force to prevent Iran from ever becoming a nuclear weapons state"?

---

to cooperate with inspectors on numerous occasions. It is therefore especially crucial that we receive explicit assurances that the Iranian regime interprets this provision as a permanent ban on ever developing nuclear weapons and that there has been a meeting of the minds on this issue.

6. How exactly will the inspections regime work?[*] Precisely how much time will the Iranians have between a request for inspection and the inspection itself? What precisely will they be permitted to do during this hiatus? And why do they need so much time if they don't plan to cheat?[†]

7. What will President Obama do if Iran is caught cheating on this deal during his administration?

8. Precisely when will which sanctions be lifted under the agreement? Do provisions that prevent the P5 plus one from imposing new sanctions apply even if Iran is found to be in violation of its commitments under

---

[*] Numerous commentators have cast doubt on the efficacy of the inspections regime envisioned by the JCPOA, in particular regarding confidential agreements between the IAEA and Iran. Several US congressmen have requested to be briefed on the content of these agreements, as has the Israeli government, but the Obama administration has been uncooperative thus far; see for example Marc Thiesen, "Obama's Secret Iran Deals Exposed," *The Washington Post*, 27 July 2015, Raphael Ahren, "Weak Inspections Regime is Nuclear Deal's Achilles Heel," *The Times of Israel*, 14 July 2015, and Barak Ravid, "Israeli Official: Powers Aren't Sharing Iran Deal Despite Promises," *Haaretz*, 29 July 2015.

[†] See Annex I, section Q, paragraph 78 in the text of the JCPOA given in Appendix 2 below. While the language is confused at best, it is clear that in the worst-case scenario, inspectors would only be able to access a given site 24 days after making the original request (14 days from the original request for access, plus 7 days of deliberations by the Joint Commission, and 3 days for Iran to implement). See also Rebecca Kaplan, "Obama Says Inspectors Get Access to 'Any' Site in Iran. Is It True?" CBS News, 14 July 2015

the agreement?* When exactly will sanctions prohibiting the sale of weapons, and particularly missile technology, be lifted?†

If and when these and other important questions about the deal are answered—directly, candidly, and unambiguously—Congress will be in a better position to answer the fundamental questions now before it: would rejecting this deeply flawed deal produce more dangerous results than not rejecting it? If so, what can we now do to assure that Iran will not acquire a nuclear arsenal? The answers to those questions may profoundly affect the future of the world.

---

* See for example paragraph 26: "the EU will refrain from re-introducing or re-imposing the sanctions that it has terminated implementing under this JCPOA…. The U.S. Administration, acting consistent with the respective roles of the President and the Congress, will refrain from re-introducing or re-imposing the sanctions specified in Annex II that it has ceased applying under this JCPOA…." *Joint Comprehensive Plan of Action*, Vienna, 14 July 2015.

† Particular attention should be paid to Annex II, which contains a list of sanctions on "Arms" that will be lifted under the agreement. *Joint Comprehensive Plan of Action*, Vienna, 14 July 2015.

A Constructive Proposal: How Congress Can Improve the Deal and Prevent Iran from Obtaining Nuclear Weapons

Congress now has the power to improve this bad deal in a way that reduces the chances that Iran will obtain a nuclear arsenal. The key lies in the words of the deal itself. In both the preface and the preamble and general provisions, the following commitment is made: "Iran reaffirms that *under no circumstances* will Iran *ever* seek, develop, or acquire any nuclear weapons" (emphasis added). This noteworthy provision is rarely mentioned by supporters of the agreement.

Congress should now enact legislation declaring that this reaffirmation is an integral part of the agreement and represents the policy of the United States. It is too late to change the words of the deal, but it is not too late for Congress to insist that Iran comply fully with its provisions.

In order to ensure that the entirety of the agreement is carried out, *including that reaffirmation*, Congress should adopt the proposal made by Thomas L. Friedman on 22 July 2015 and by myself on 5 September 2013. To quote Friedman: "Congress should pass a resolution authorizing this and future presidents to use force to prevent Iran from ever becoming a nuclear weapons state.... Iran must know now that the U.S. president is authorized to destroy—without warning or negotiation—any attempt by Tehran to build a bomb."[*]

The benefits of enacting such legislation are clear: the law would underline the centrality to the deal of Iran's reaffirmation never to acquire nuclear weapons, and would provide both a deterrent against Iran violating its reaffirmation and an enforcement authorization in the event it does.

I am confident that there would be enough votes both in the Senate and House to pass such a law. Were President Obama to veto it, he would be hard pressed to explain his opposition to a law that accepted the language of the deal itself at face value, and that reiterated his own statements that the military option remains on the table. Moreover, a presidential veto of this forward-looking law would have a far better chance of being overridden by Congress than would the veto of a law that simply rejected the deal without offering any alternative.

This deal's proponents argue that critics never offer better alternatives to what is now on the table. Well, this constructive alternative to simply accepting or rejecting the current deal provides a backstop against its worst-case scenario, while preserving the benefits of the agreement. A law based on these two

---

[*] Thomas Friedman, "Backing Up Our Wager with Iran," *New York Times*, 22 July 2015. This is the way I put it back in 2013: "President Obama should ask Congress for authorization now to take military action against Iran's nuclear weapons program if it were to cross the red line he has already drawn. If Congress gives its approval, that action will increase the deterrent threat currently directed against Iran, by underscoring the red line as having been drawn both by the president and by Congress. It should leave no doubt in the minds of the Iranian mullahs that the president not only has the will to enforce the red line but also has the authority from Congress to do so." See Chapter IV, B. supra.

elements—adopting Iran's reaffirmation as the official American policy and authorizing a tough response if Iran tries to obtain nuclear weapons—may be an alternative we can live with, whether the deal is accepted or rejected. But without such an alternative or supplement, the deal as currently written will not prevent Iran from obtaining nuclear weapons. In all probability, it would merely postpone that catastrophe for about a decade while legitimating its occurrence. This is not an outcome we can live with.

Timeline of the Iranian Nuclear Program
and Ensuing Negotiations[131]

1. *1957–1979: Birth of the Iranian Nuclear Program:*
   Atoms for Peace

In 1957, Iran launches a civilian nuclear program with the assistance of the United States through the Cooperation Concerning Civil Uses of Atoms, part of the Wbroader Atoms for Peace initiative promoted by the Eisenhower administration. Throughout the 1960s and 1970s the US provides Iran with nuclear technology and materials, including a 5-megawatt nuclear research reactor and highly enriched uranium in 1967. The Atoms for Peace program also allows Iranian scientists to receive nuclear education and training in the United States, which in turn leads to the foundation of the Atomic Energy Organization of Iran (AEOI). In 1968, Iran ratifies the Nuclear Non-Proliferation Treaty, pledging to never become a nuclear-weapon state. By 1976, the AEOI is receiving $1 billion in annual funding, and offers specialized master's programs in nuclear energy, in cooperation with MIT.

2. *1979–2002: The Islamic Republic and Secret Pursuit of a Nuclear Weapon*

With the fall of the Shah in January 1979, the US stops providing enriched uranium for the Tehran research reactor, and ceases all cooperation with Iran in February when Ayatollah Khomeini comes to power. Khomeini, uninterested in the Shah's nuclear initiative, decides to shut down the program altogether. However, the Iran-Iraq war and Saddam Hussein's pursuit of a nuclear weapon causes the new regime to reconsider. With the help of the Pakistani scientist Abdul Qadeer Khan, Iran acquires uranium enrichment technology, and in 1995, the new supreme leader, Ayatollah Ali Khameni, announces an $800 million contract with Russia to complete two nuclear facilities. Publicly, Khameni supports Saudi initiatives to rid the Middle East of nuclear weapons, and in 2003 he supports a Syrian proposal to that effect. However, in 2002, an Iranian dissident shares documents revealing that Iran has been secretly pursuing a nuclear weapons program, including the construction of an enrichment plant and a heavy water plant. Iran subsequently agrees to inspections by the International Atomic Energy Association ("IAEA"), while simultaneously working with Russia to speed up the construction of a nuclear power plant at Bushehr.

3. *2003–2006: First Negotiations with Iran: EU 3 and P5+1*

In June 2003, the IAEA concludes that Iran has breached its obligations under the Nuclear Non-Proliferation Treaty after Iran denies inspectors full access to the Natanz nuclear production facility in May. Later, in June, the United Kingdom, Germany, and France (the "EU 3") begin diplomatic efforts to address Iran's nuclear policy, without US cooperation. These negotiations, coupled with the threat of referral to United Nations Security Council and the ongoing US occupation of Iraq, convince Khameni to cooperate with the IAEA and to suspend uranium enrichment in October 2003. However, in 2005, the election of new Iranian Prime Minister Mahmoud Ahmadinejad causes the EU 3 talks to collapse and in September, Ahmadinejad delivers a speech at the UN where he states that Iran has the right to pursue nuclear weapons. In January 2006, he authorizes the resumption of uranium enrichment activities. In response, in February 2006 the IAEA refers Iran to the Security Council, and in July the Security Council passes its first resolution demanding that Iran cease enriching and processing uranium. Meanwhile, in June, China, the US, and Russia join the EU 3 to form the P5+1 with the aim of pressuring Iran to abandon its nuclear ambitions.

4. *2006–2010: Expansion of Iran's Nuclear Program, Birth of the International Sanctions Regime, Sabotage Efforts, and Threats of Israeli Military Intervention*

In August 2006, Ahmadinejad inaugurates a heavy water production plant at Arak capable of producing weapons-grade plutonium. In response, in December the Security Council passes the first of six resolutions imposing gradual sanctions on Iran, including the freezing of assets of individuals and companies affiliated with uranium enrichment and reprocessing. Simultaneously, the US ramps up cyber attacks on the Iranian nuclear infrastructure; these attacks eventually cause a major crash at the Natanz nuclear plant, destroying thousands of centrifuges, and setting the Iranian program back several years. In 2008, George W. Bush refuses Israeli requests for specialized bunker-busting bombs, fearing the consequences of a preemptive Israeli strike on Iranian nuclear facilities. In April 2009, the US joins with the other P5+1 countries in negotiations with Iran, headed by then–Secretary of State Hilary Clinton. Following the disclosure by UN inspectors in February 2010 of evidence that Iran has been secretly pursuing a nuclear warhead, the UN levels new sanctions and enforcement measures, and the US passes the Comprehensive Iran Sanctions, Accountability, and Divestment Act in June. Meanwhile, Israel is suspected of carrying out several assassinations of Iranian nuclear scientists, most notably in November 2010, when Majid Shahari, a prominent figure in the IAEO, is killed by a bomb. Similar attacks continue into 2012.

5. *November 2011: Europe Imposes Sanctions, the Iranian Nuclear Program Recovers*

In November, the European Union and many major European nations impose sanctions targeted at Iran's central and commercial banks, in order to isolate Iran from the international financial system. The United States simultaneously imposes sanctions on companies involved in Iran's nuclear, petrochemical, and oil industries. Meanwhile, the United Nations atomic agency releases evidence that "Iran has carried out activities relevant to the development of a nuclear device..." at its Parchin military base. In Iran, the Natanz nuclear plant recovers from a cyber attack, reportedly initiated by the United States, and resumes enriching uranium.

6. *March–August 2012: More Centrifuges, Negotiations Falter*

In March 2012, Iran announces that it is building about 3,000 advanced uranium-enrichment centrifuges at the Natanz plant. IAEA inspectors are denied access to the Parchin facility south of Tehran, where they are seeking information regarding Iran's attempts to build a nuclear trigger. In May, talks between the P5+1 and Iran in Baghdad fail to produce a breakthrough; the diplomatic situation worsens when the P5+1 refuse to ease sanctions, and the IAEA releases a statement that Iran has made no progress towards providing inspectors access to restricted sites it suspects are being used to develop nuclear warheads. In July, the European Union imposes sanctions similar to those authorized by the US in 2011, restricting Iran's ability to export and sell oil. Iran's oil minister later admits that US and EU sanctions cause Iranian oil prices to drop by 40%, costing the Iranian government between $4 and $8 billion each month. In August, the US intensifies sanctions on Iran's oil, petrochemical, and shipping industries. Meanwhile, Iran continues to upgrade its nuclear capabilities, installing centrifuges at a deep-underground site under a mountain near Qom.

7. *September 2012–February 2013: Israel's Red Line,
   Iran's Currency Crisis, and Further Sanctions*

In September, Prime Minister Benjamin Netanyahu of Israel delivers a speech at the United Nations in which he warns that Iran will soon be able to manufacture a nuclear weapon. Meanwhile, Iran's currency tumbles as a result of EU- and US-led sanctions: by October the rial has lost over 50% of its value since the beginning of the year. The Iranian government fears that the central bank will not be able to print enough money to keep up with ongoing currency devaluation, and arrests several money traders to limit speculation that inflation will render the rial worthless. That same month, the EU strengthens sanctions, targeting the Iranian metal and natural gas industries, and making business transactions more cumbersome. Following Iran's announcement that it would deploy a new generation of centrifuges at the end of January 2013, the US passes further sanctions restricting Iran's ability to repatriate money generated from foreign transactions.

8. *March–May 2013: Threats of Military Action,
   Sanctions' Continued Impact*

In an interview with an Israeli television station in March, President Obama says that Iran is at least a year away from developing nuclear weapons. In April, Israeli officials including Prime Minister Netanyahu emphasize Israel's willingness to initiate military action against the Iranian nuclear program unilaterally. The same month, Iran announces an expansion in its uranium production after talks with the P5+1 in Kazakhstan stall. The

US responds first by blacklisting several businessmen accused of violating the sanctions regime, and then by announcing arms agreements with the United Arab Emirates, Saudi Arabia, and Israel to help those countries counter any potential Iranian military threat. In Iran, the price of staple goods has risen by over 60% causing many Iranians to stockpile basic essentials in large quantities, fearing a further reduction in their spending power due to inflation. In May, the US expands sanctions again, targeting Iranian businesses, individuals and corporations aiding Iran, companies controlled by Iran's leadership, and freezing Iranian assets located in the United States. These measures are augmented the following month by restrictions against the automotive industry, and foreign banks that hold or trade the Iranian currency. Nonetheless, the IAEA warns that Iran's nuclear program is continuing to advance, and that its heavy water plant at Arak might be fully operational by the end of 2014.

9. *June 2013–January 2014: A New Iranian President and Progress in Negotiations*

Following the election of the more moderate Hassan Rouhani as Iranian Prime Minister in June 2013, negotiations make substantial progress. In August, Iran slows its gathering of uranium; in September, Mr. Rouhani appears at the United Nations and states that nuclear weapons have no place in his country's future. That same month, Iran and the United States engage in direct talks for the first time since 1979. In November, negotiations yield a breakthrough: first, on November 11, Iran announces that it has agreed to a 'road map' with UN inspectors to visit the Parchin site. Then, on November 24, the P5+1 announce that they have reached an agreement to halt Iran's nuclear program for 6 months, as part of the groundwork for a broader permanent agreement.

10. *January–November 2014: Setting the Groundwork for a Permanent Agreement*

In January, despite opposition from the Israeli government and hardliners in Iran, Iran and the P5+1 agree to a deal whereby Iran will receive limited sanctions relief and, in exchange, cease activity on its nuclear program. In May, the IAEA confirms that Iran has been cooperating to provide information regarding the function of nuclear detonators, and in July, Iran agrees to the general framework for a permanent agreement: Iran will cease enriching uranium for several years, while receiving progressive sanctions relief. Major differences remain between the negotiating parties—primarily as regards how much of its nuclear infrastructure Iran will have to dismantle—and as a result, talks are extended for an additional four months. While there is very little substantive progress made during that time period, Iran begins to repurpose part of the Arak nuclear facility to limit its output of plutonium, thereby hoping to curry favor with the P5+1. By the time the self-imposed November deadline looms, there have been several important breakthroughs: Iran has agreed to ship much of its highly enriched uranium to Russia for conversion into specialized fuel rods for the power plant at Bushehr. Nonetheless, the parties decide to extend negotiations by another seven months to resolve outstanding differences.

11. *November 2014–July 2015: Closing the Deal*

After months of negotiations, Iran agrees to several limits on its nuclear program and a provisional framework is agreed upon with the P5+1. In particular, Iran agrees to halve the number of operational centrifuges, limit the operations of several of its nuclear sites, including the heavy water plant at Arak and the underground facility at Fordo. In return, the European Union and the United States will begin to lift sanctions, as Iran complies with the terms of the agreement. These provisions remain largely unaltered in the final text of the deal, which is released on 14 July 2015, and whose text can be found below.

APPENDIX 2

JOINT COMPREHENSIVE PLAN OF ACTION

Vienna, 14 July 2015

*The following is an abridged text of the JCPOA, with **commentary** by Alan Dershowitz.*

PREFACE

The E3/EU+3 (China, France, Germany, the Russian Federation, the United Kingdom and the United States, with the High Representative of the European Union for Foreign Affairs and Security Policy) and the Islamic Republic of Iran welcome this historic Joint Comprehensive Plan of Action (JCPOA), which will ensure that Iran's nuclear programme will be exclusively peaceful, and mark a fundamental shift in their approach to this issue. They anticipate that full implementation of this JCPOA will positively contribute to regional and international peace and security. Iran reaffirms that under no circumstances will Iran ever seek, develop or acquire any nuclear weapons. *[Is this last sentence a binding, enforceable part of the deal? If so, why has it not been emphasized by its supporters?]*

Iran envisions that this JCPOA will allow it to move forward with an exclusively peaceful, indigenous nuclear programme, in line with scientific and economic considerations, in accordance with the JCPOA, and with a view to building confidence and encouraging international cooperation. In this context, the initial mutually determined limitations described in this JCPOA will be followed by a gradual evolution, at a reasonable pace, of Iran's peaceful nuclear programme, including its enrichment activities, to a commercial programme for exclusively peaceful purposes, consistent with international non-proliferation norms.

The E3/EU+3 envision that the implementation of this JCPOA will progressively allow them to gain confidence in the exclusively peaceful nature of Iran's programme. The JCPOA reflects mutually determined parameters, consistent with practical needs, with agreed limits on the scope of Iran's nuclear programme, including enrichment activities and R&D. The JCPOA addresses the E3/EU+3's concerns, including through comprehensive measures providing for transparency and verification.

The JCPOA will produce the comprehensive lifting of all UN Security Council sanctions as well as multilateral and national sanctions related to Iran's nuclear programme, including steps on access in areas of trade, technology, finance, and energy.

PREAMBLE AND GENERAL PROVISIONS

[Are the provisions contained in this section, and particularly Article iii., operative elements of the agreement? Are they binding and enforceable?]

i. The Islamic Republic of Iran and the E3/EU+3 (China, France, Germany, the Russian Federation, the United Kingdom and the United States, with the High Representative of the European Union for Foreign Affairs and Security Policy) have decided upon this long-term Joint Comprehensive Plan of Action (JCPOA). This JCPOA, reflecting a step-by-step approach, includes the reciprocal commitments as laid down in this document and the annexes hereto and is to be endorsed by the United Nations (UN) Security Council.

ii. The full implementation of this JCPOA will ensure the exclusively peaceful nature of Iran's nuclear programme.

iii. Iran reaffirms that under no circumstances will Iran ever seek, develop or acquire any nuclear weapons.

iv. Successful implementation of this JCPOA will enable Iran to fully enjoy its right to nuclear energy for peaceful purposes under the relevant articles of the nuclear Non-Proliferation Treaty (NPT) in line with its obligations therein, and the Iranian nuclear programme will be treated in the same manner as that of any other non-nuclear-weapon state party to the NPT.

v. This JCPOA will produce the comprehensive lifting of all UN Security Council sanctions as well as multilateral and national sanctions related to Iran's nuclear programme, including steps on access in areas of trade, technology, finance and energy.

vi. The E3/EU+3 and Iran reaffirm their commitment to the purposes and principles of the United Nations as set out in the UN Charter.

vii. The E3/EU+3 and Iran acknowledge that the NPT remains the cornerstone of the nuclear non-proliferation regime and the essential foundation for the pursuit of nuclear disarmament and for the peaceful uses of nuclear energy.

viii. The E3/EU+3 and Iran commit to implement this JCPOA in good faith and in a constructive atmosphere, based on mutual respect, and to refrain from any action inconsistent with the letter, spirit and intent of this JCPOA that would undermine its successful implementation. The E3/EU+3 will refrain from imposing discriminatory regulatory and procedural requirements in lieu of the sanctions and restrictive measures covered by this JCPOA. This JCPOA builds on the implementation of the Joint Plan of Action (JPOA) agreed in Geneva on 24 November 2013.

ix. A Joint Commission consisting of the E3/EU+3 and Iran will be established to monitor the implementation of this JCPOA and will carry out the functions provided for in this JCPOA. This Joint Commission will address issues arising from the implementation of this JCPOA and will operate in accordance with the provisions as detailed in the relevant annex.

x. The International Atomic Energy Agency (IAEA) will be requested to monitor and verify the voluntary nuclear-related measures as detailed in this JCPOA. The IAEA will be requested to provide regular updates to the Board of Governors, and as provided for in this JCPOA, to the UN Security Council. All relevant rules and regulations of the IAEA with regard to the protection of information will be fully observed by all parties involved.

xi. All provisions and measures contained in this JCPOA are only for the purpose of its implementation between E3/EU+3 and Iran and should not be considered as setting precedents for any other state or for fundamental principles of international law and the rights and obligations under the NPT and other relevant instruments, as well as for internationally recognised principles and practices.

xii. Technical details of the implementation of this JCPOA are dealt with in the annexes to this document.

xiii. The EU and E3+3 countries and Iran, in the framework of the JCPOA, will cooperate, as appropriate, in the field of peaceful uses of nuclear energy and engage in mutually determined civil nuclear cooperation projects as detailed in Annex III, including through IAEA involvement.

xiv. The E3+3 will submit a draft resolution to the UN Security Council endorsing this JCPOA affirming that conclusion of this JCPOA marks a fundamental shift in its consideration of this issue and expressing its desire to build a new relationship with Iran. This UN Security Council resolution will also provide for the termination on Implementation Day of provisions imposed under previous resolutions; establishment of specific restrictions; and conclusion of consideration of the Iran nuclear issue by the UN Security Council 10 years after the Adoption Day. *[This provision does not specify when the resolutions should be submitted and voted on, yet the United States agreed to it before Congress had the opportunity to consider the deal.]*

xv. The provisions stipulated in this JCPOA will be implemented for their respective durations as set forth below and detailed in the annexes.

xvi. The E3/EU+3 and Iran will meet at the ministerial level every 2 years, or earlier if needed, in order to review and assess progress and to adopt appropriate decisions by consensus.

I. Iran and E3/EU+3 will take the following voluntary measures within the timeframe as detailed in this JCPOA and its Annexes

[Why are they being called "voluntary" if they are binding provisions of a formal, binding agreement?]

NUCLEAR

A. *Enrichment, Enrichment R&D, Stockpiles*

1. Iran's long term plan includes certain agreed limitations on all uranium enrichment and uranium enrichment-related activities including certain limitations on specific research and development (R&D) activities for the first 8 years, to be followed by gradual evolution, at a reasonable pace, to the next stage of its enrichment activities for exclusively peaceful purposes, as described in Annex I. Iran will abide by its voluntary commitments, as expressed in its own long-term enrichment and enrichment R&D plan to be submitted as part of the initial declaration for the Additional Protocol to Iran's Safeguards Agreement. *[Note that these limitations expire in eight years. Why so soon?]*

2. Iran will begin phasing out its IR-1 centrifuges in 10 years. During this period, Iran will keep its enrichment capacity at Natanz at up to a total installed uranium enrichment capacity of 5060 IR-1 centrifuges. Excess centrifuges and enrichment-related infrastructure at Natanz will be stored under IAEA continuous monitoring, as specified in Annex I. *[This obligation begins in ten years, thus creating a two-year hiatus with the prior eight-year limitation.]*

3. Iran will continue to conduct enrichment R&D in a manner that does not accumulate enriched uranium. Iran's enrichment R&D with

uranium for 10 years will only include IR-4, IR-5, IR-6 and IR-8 centrifuges as laid out in Annex I, and Iran will not engage in other isotope separation technologies for enrichment of uranium as specified in Annex I. Iran will continue testing IR-6 and IR-8 centrifuges, and will commence testing of up to 30 IR-6 and IR-8 centrifuges after eight and a half years, as detailed in Annex I.

4. As Iran will be phasing out its IR-1 centrifuges, it will not manufacture or assemble other centrifuges, except as provided for in Annex I, and will replace failed centrifuges with centrifuges of the same type. Iran will manufacture advanced centrifuge machines only for the purposes specified in this JCPOA. From the end of the eighth year, and as described in Annex I, Iran will start to manufacture agreed numbers of IR-6 and IR-8 centrifuge machines without rotors and will store all of the manufactured machines at Natanz, under IAEA continuous monitoring until they are needed under Iran's long-term enrichment and enrichment R&D plan. *[What does "continuous monitoring" actually entail?]*

5. Based on its long-term plan, for 15 years, Iran will carry out its uranium enrichment-related activities, including safeguarded R&D exclusively in the Natanz Enrichment facility, keep its level of uranium enrichment at up to 3.67%, and, at Fordow, refrain from any uranium enrichment and uranium enrichment R&D and from keeping any nuclear material. *[This is limited to fifteen years. After that, can it engage in activities that are military in nature?]*

6. Iran will convert the Fordow facility into a nuclear, physics and technology centre. International collaboration including in the form of scientific joint partnerships will be established in agreed areas of research. 1044 IR-1 centrifuges in six cascades will remain in one wing at Fordow. Two of these cascades will spin without uranium and will be transitioned, including through appropriate infrastructure modification, for stable isotope production. The other four cascades with all

associated infrastructure will remain idle. All other centrifuges and enrichment-related infrastructure will be removed and stored under IAEA continuous monitoring as specified in Annex I.

7. During the 15 year period, and as Iran gradually moves to meet international qualification standards for nuclear fuel produced in Iran, it will keep its uranium stockpile under 300 kg of up to 3.67% enriched uranium hexafluoride (UF6) or the equivalent in other chemical forms. The excess quantities are to be sold based on international prices and delivered to the international buyer in return for natural uranium delivered to Iran, or are to be down-blended to natural uranium level. Enriched uranium in fabricated fuel assemblies from Russia or other sources for use in Iran's nuclear reactors will not be counted against the above stated 300 kg UF6 stockpile, if the criteria set out in Annex I are met with regard to other sources. The Joint Commission will support assistance to Iran, including through IAEA technical cooperation as appropriate, in meeting international qualification standards for nuclear fuel produced in Iran. All remaining uranium oxide enriched to between 5% and 20% will be fabricated into fuel for the Tehran Research Reactor (TRR). Any additional fuel needed for the TRR will be made available to Iran at international market prices. *[This seems positive.]*

B. Arak, Heavy Water, Reprocessing

8. Iran will redesign and rebuild a modernised heavy water research reactor in Arak, based on an agreed conceptual design, using fuel enriched up to 3.67 %, in a form of an international partnership which will certify the final design. The reactor will support peaceful nuclear research and radioisotope production for medical and industrial purposes. The redesigned and rebuilt Arak reactor will not produce weapons grade

plutonium. Except for the first core load, all of the activities for redesigning and manufacturing of the fuel assemblies for the redesigned reactor will be carried out in Iran. All spent fuel from Arak will be shipped out of Iran for the lifetime of the reactor. This international partnership will include participating E3/EU+3 parties, Iran and such other countries as may be mutually determined. Iran will take the leadership role as the owner and as the project manager and the E3/ EU+3 and Iran will, before Implementation Day, conclude an official document which would define the responsibilities assumed by the E3/ EU+3 participants. *[This seems positive.]*

9.   Iran plans to keep pace with the trend of international technological advancement in relying on light water for its future power and research reactors with enhanced international cooperation, including assurance of supply of necessary fuel.

10.   There will be no additional heavy water reactors or accumulation of heavy water in Iran for 15 years. All excess heavy water will be made available for export to the international market. *[Why a fifteen-year limitation on heavy water?]*

11.   Iran intends to ship out all spent fuel for all future and present power and research nuclear reactors, for further treatment or disposition as provided for in relevant contracts to be duly concluded with the recipient party. *["Iran intends" does not sound binding. Why not say "Iran will not, and does not intend..." as in the next paragraph?]*

12.   For 15 years Iran will not, and does not intend to thereafter, engage in any spent fuel reprocessing or construction of a facility capable of spent fuel reprocessing, or reprocessing R&D activities leading to a spent fuel reprocessing capability, with the sole exception of separation activities aimed exclusively at the production of medical and industrial radio-isotopes from irradiated enriched uranium targets. *[Why 15 years?]*

C. *Transparency and Confidence Building Measures*

13.   Consistent with the respective roles of the President and Majlis (Parliament), Iran will provisionally apply the Additional Protocol to its Comprehensive Safeguards Agreement in accordance with Article 17(b) of the Additional Protocol, proceed with its ratification within the timeframe as detailed in Annex V and fully implement the modified Code 3.1 of the Subsidiary Arrangements to its Safeguards Agreement.

14.   Iran will fully implement the "Roadmap for Clarification of Past and Present Outstanding Issues" agreed with the IAEA, containing arrangements to address past and present issues of concern relating to its nuclear programme as raised in the annex to the IAEA report of 8 November 2011 (GOV/2011/65). Full implementation of activities undertaken under the Roadmap by Iran will be completed by 15 October 2015, and subsequently the Director General will provide by 15 December 2015 the final assessment on the resolution of all past and present outstanding issues to the Board of Governors, and the E3+3, in their capacity as members of the Board of Governors, will submit a resolution to the Board of Governors for taking necessary action, with a view to closing the issue, without prejudice to the competence of the Board of Governors.

15.   Iran will allow the IAEA to monitor the implementation of the voluntary measures for their respective durations, as well as to implement transparency measures, as set out in this JCPOA and its Annexes. These measures include: a long-term IAEA presence in Iran; IAEA monitoring of uranium ore concentrate produced by Iran from all uranium ore concentrate plants for 25 years; containment and surveillance of centrifuge rotors and bellows for 20 years; use of IAEA approved and certified modern technologies including on-line enrichment measurement and electronic seals; and a reliable mechanism

to ensure speedy resolution of IAEA access concerns for 15 years, as defined in Annex I. *[What precisely are these "speedy resolution" measures, and will they ensure effective inspections?]*

16. Iran will not engage in activities, including at the R&D level, that could contribute to the development of a nuclear explosive device, including uranium or plutonium metallurgy activities, as specified in Annex I. *[This seems positive, if enforced.]*

17. Iran will cooperate and act in accordance with the procurement channel in this JCPOA, as detailed in Annex IV, endorsed by the UN Security Council resolution.

SANCTIONS

18.   The UN Security Council resolution endorsing this JCPOA will terminate all provisions of previous UN Security Council resolutions on the
Iranian nuclear issue - 1696 (2006), 1737 (2006), 1747 (2007), 1803
(2008), 1835 (2008), 1929 (2010) and 2224 (2015) – simultaneously
with the IAEA-verified implementation of agreed nuclear-related
measures by Iran and will establish specific restrictions, as specified
in Annex V.[1]

19.   The EU will terminate all provisions of the EU Regulation, as subsequently amended, implementing all nuclear-related economic and
financial sanctions, including related designations, simultaneously
with the IAEA-verified implementation of agreed nuclear-related
measures by Iran as specified in Annex V, which cover all sanctions and
restrictive measures in the following areas, as described in Annex II:

i.   Transfers of funds between EU persons and entities, including financial institutions, and Iranian persons and entities, including financial
institutions; *[This is a major sanction.]*

ii.   Banking activities, including the establishment of new correspondent
banking relationships and the opening of new branches and subsidiar-
ies of Iranian banks in the territories of EU Member States;

iii. Provision of insurance and reinsurance;

iv.   Supply of specialised financial messaging services, including SWIFT, for persons and entities set out in Attachment 1 to Annex II, including the Central Bank of Iran and Iranian financial institutions;

v.   Financial support for trade with Iran (export credit, guarantees or insurance);

vi.   Commitments for grants, financial assistance and concessional loans to the Government of Iran;

vii.   Transactions in public or public-guaranteed bonds;

viii.   Import and transport of Iranian oil, petroleum products, gas and petrochemical products;

ix.   Export of key equipment or technology for the oil, gas and petrochemical sectors;

x.   Investment in the oil, gas and petrochemical sectors;

xi.   Export of key naval equipment and technology;

xii.   Design and construction of cargo vessels and oil tankers;

xiii.   Provision of flagging and classification services;

xiv.   Access to EU airports of Iranian cargo flights;

xv.   Export of gold, precious metals and diamonds;

xvi.   Delivery of Iranian banknotes and coinage;

xvii.   Export of graphite, raw or semi-finished metals such as aluminum and steel, and export or software for integrating industrial processes;

xviii.   Designation of persons, entities and bodies (asset freeze and visa ban) set out in Attachment 1 to Annex II; and

xix.   Associated services for each of the categories above.

20.   The EU will terminate all provisions of the EU Regulation implementing all EU proliferation-related sanctions, including related designations, 8 years after Adoption Day or when the IAEA has reached the Broader Conclusion that all nuclear material in Iran remains in peaceful activities, whichever is earlier. *[This provides considerable wiggle room.]*

21.   The United States will cease the application, and will continue to do so, in accordance with this JCPOA of the sanctions specified in Annex II to take effect simultaneously with the IAEA-verified implementation of the agreed nuclear-related measures by Iran as specified in Annex V. Such sanctions cover the following areas as described in Annex II:

i.   Financial and banking transactions with Iranian banks and financial institutions as specified in Annex II, including the Central Bank of Iran and specified individuals and entities identified as Government of Iran by the Office of Foreign Assets Control on the Specially Designated Nationals and Blocked Persons List (SDN List), as set out in Attachment 3 to Annex II (including the opening and maintenance of correspondent and payable through-accounts at non-U.S. financial institutions, investments, foreign exchange transactions and letters of credit);

ii.   Transactions in Iranian Rial;

iii.   Provision of U.S. banknotes to the Government of Iran;

iv.   Bilateral trade limitations on Iranian revenues abroad, including limitations on their transfer;

v.   Purchase, subscription to, or facilitation of the issuance of Iranian sovereign debt, including governmental bonds;

vi.   Financial messaging services to the Central Bank of Iran and Iranian financial institutions set out in Attachment 3 to Annex II;

vii.   Underwriting services, insurance, or reinsurance;

viii. Efforts to reduce Iran's crude oil sales;

ix.   Investment, including participation in joint ventures, goods, services, information, technology and technical expertise and support for Iran's oil, gas and petrochemical sectors;

x.   Purchase, acquisition, sale, transportation or marketing of petroleum, petrochemical products and natural gas from Iran;

xi.   Export, sale or provision of refined petroleum products and petrochemical products to Iran;

xii.   Transactions with Iran's energy sector;

xiii.   Transactions with Iran's shipping and shipbuilding sectors and port operators;

xiv.   Trade in gold and other precious metals;

xv.   Trade with Iran in graphite, raw or semi-finished metals such as aluminum and steel, coal, and software for integrating industrial processes;

xvi.   Sale, supply or transfer of goods and services used in connection with Iran's automotive sector;

xvii.   Sanctions on associated services for each of the categories above;

xviii.   Remove individuals and entities set out in Attachment 3 to Annex II from the SDN List, the Foreign Sanctions Evaders List, and/or the Non-SDN Iran Sanctions Act List; and

xix.   Terminate Executive Orders 13574, 13590, 13622, and 13645, and Sections 5 – 7 and 15 of Executive Order 13628. [The president has no constitutional power to end congressionally imposed sanctions without a law passed by Congress. Since the president has said that this agreement is not a treaty, it does not have the force of law and cannot compel Congress to take any action.]

22.   The United States will, as specified in Annex II and in accordance with Annex V, allow for the sale of commercial passenger aircraft and related parts and services to Iran; license non-U.S. persons that are owned or controlled by a U.S. person to engage in activities with Iran consistent with this JCPOA; and license the importation into the United States of Iranian-origin carpets and foodstuffs.

23.   Eight years after Adoption Day or when the IAEA has reached the Broader Conclusion that all nuclear material in Iran remains in peaceful activities, whichever is earlier, the United States will seek such legislative action as may be appropriate to terminate, or modify to effectuate the termination of, the sanctions specified in Annex II on the acquisition of nuclear-related commodities and services for nuclear

activities contemplated in this JCPOA, to be consistent with the U.S. approach to other non-nuclear-weapon states under the NPT.

24.   The E3/EU and the United States specify in Annex II a full and complete list of all nuclear-related sanctions or restrictive measures and will lift them in accordance with Annex V. Annex II also specifies the effects of the lifting of sanctions beginning on "Implementation Day". If at any time following the Implementation Day, Iran believes that any other nuclear-related sanction or restrictive measure of the E3/EU+3 is preventing the full implementation of the sanctions lifting as specified in this JCPOA, the JCPOA participant in question will consult with Iran with a view to resolving the issue and, if they concur that lifting of this sanction or restrictive measure is appropriate, the JCPOA participant in question will take appropriate action. If they are not able to resolve the issue, Iran or any member of the E3/EU+3 may refer the issue to the Joint Commission.

25.   If a law at the state or local level in the United States is preventing the implementation of the sanctions lifting as specified in this JCPOA, the United States will take appropriate steps, taking into account all available authorities, with a view to achieving such implementation. The United States will actively encourage officials at the state or local level to take into account the changes in the U.S. policy reflected in the lifting of sanctions under this JCPOA and to refrain from actions inconsistent with this change in policy. *[This agreement does not reflect "changes in the U.S. policy" regarding sanctions. It only reflects the policy of the executive branch. That is the problem with sole executive agreements. The president can't have it both ways.]*

26.   The EU will refrain from re-introducing or re-imposing the sanctions that it has terminated implementing under this JCPOA, without prejudice to the dispute resolution process provided for under this JCPOA. There will be no new nuclear- related UN Security Council sanctions and no new EU nuclear-related sanctions or restrictive

measures. The United States will make best efforts in good faith to sustain this JCPOA and to prevent interference with the realisation of the full benefit by Iran of the sanctions lifting specified in Annex II. The U.S. Administration, acting consistent with the respective roles of the President and the Congress, will refrain from re-introducing or re-imposing the sanctions specified in Annex II that it has ceased applying under this JCPOA, without prejudice to the dispute resolution process provided for under this JCPOA. The U.S. Administration, acting consistent with the respective roles of the President and the Congress, will refrain from imposing new nuclear-related sanctions. Iran has stated that it will treat such a re-introduction or re-imposition of the sanctions specified in Annex II, or such an imposition of new nuclear-related sanctions, as grounds to cease performing its commitments under this JCPOA in whole or in part. *[This provision gives Iran an easy way out of complying with its obligations under the deal. If Congress decides to impose nuclear-related sanctions, Iran has the right "to cease performing its commitments under this JCPOA in whole or in part." This is a potentially dangerous provision.]*

27. The E3/EU+3 will take adequate administrative and regulatory measures to ensure clarity and effectiveness with respect to the lifting of sanctions under this JCPOA. The EU and its Member States as well as the United States will issue relevant guidelines and make publicly accessible statements on the details of sanctions or restrictive measures which have been lifted under this JCPOA. The EU and its Member States and the United States commit to consult with Iran regarding the content of such guidelines and statements, on a regular basis and whenever appropriate.

28. The E3/EU+3 and Iran commit to implement this JCPOA in good faith and in a constructive atmosphere, based on mutual respect, and to refrain from any action inconsistent with the letter, spirit and intent of this JCPOA that would undermine its successful implementation.

Senior Government officials of the E3/EU+3 and Iran will make every effort to support the successful implementation of this JCPOA including in their public statements. The E3/EU+3 will take all measures required to lift sanctions and will refrain from imposing exceptional or discriminatory regulatory and procedural requirements in lieu of the sanctions and restrictive measures covered by the JCPOA.

29.   The EU and its Member States and the United States, consistent with their respective laws, will refrain from any policy specifically intended to directly and adversely affect the normalisation of trade and economic relations with Iran inconsistent with their commitments not to undermine the successful implementation of this JCPOA.

30.   The E3/EU+3 will not apply sanctions or restrictive measures to persons or entities for engaging in activities covered by the lifting of sanctions provided for in this JCPOA, provided that such activities are otherwise consistent with E3/EU+3 laws and regulations in effect. Following the lifting of sanctions under this JCPOA as specified in Annex II, ongoing investigations on possible infringements of such sanctions may be reviewed in accordance with applicable national laws.

31.   Consistent with the timing specified in Annex V, the EU and its Member States will terminate the implementation of the measures applicable to designated entities and individuals, including the Central Bank of Iran and other Iranian banks and financial institutions, as detailed in Annex II and the attachments thereto. Consistent with the timing specified in Annex V, the United States will remove designation of certain entities and individuals on the Specially Designated Nationals and Blocked Persons List, and entities and individuals listed on the Foreign Sanctions Evaders List, as detailed in Annex II and the attachments thereto.

32.   EU and E3+3 countries and international participants will engage in joint projects with Iran, including through IAEA technical cooperation projects, in the field of peaceful nuclear technology, including

nuclear power plants, research reactors, fuel fabrication, agreed joint advanced R&D such as fusion, establishment of a state-of-the-art regional nuclear medical centre, personnel training, nuclear safety and security, and environmental protection, as detailed in Annex III. They will take necessary measures, as appropriate, for the implementation of these projects.

33. The E3/EU+3 and Iran will agree on steps to ensure Iran's access in areas of trade, technology, finance and energy. The EU will further explore possible areas for cooperation between the EU, its Member States and Iran, and in this context consider the use of available instruments such as export credits to facilitate trade, project financing and investment in Iran.

IMPLEMENTATION   PLAN

34.   Iran and the E3/EU+3 will implement their JCPOA commitments according to the sequence specified in Annex V. The milestones for implementation are as follows:

i.   Finalisation Day is the date on which negotiations of this JCPOA are concluded among the E3/EU+3 and Iran, to be followed promptly by submission of the resolution endorsing this JCPOA to the UN Security Council for adoption without delay. *["Without delay" should not preclude time for Congress to consider it.]*

ii.   Adoption Day is the date 90 days after the endorsement of this JCPOA by the UN Security Council, or such earlier date as may be determined by mutual consent of the JCPOA participants, at which time this JCPOA and the commitments in this JCPOA come into effect. Beginning on that date, JCPOA participants will make necessary arrangements and preparations for the implementation of their JCPOA commitments.

iii.   Implementation Day is the date on which, simultaneously with the IAEA report verifying implementation by Iran of the nuclear-related measures described in Sections 15.1. to 15.11 of Annex V, the EU and the United States take the actions described in Sections 16 and 17 of Annex V respectively and in accordance with the UN Security Council resolution, the actions described in Section 18 of Annex V occur at the UN level.

iv.   Transition Day is the date 8 years after Adoption Day or the date on which the Director General of the IAEA submits a report stating that the IAEA has reached the Broader Conclusion that all nuclear material in Iran remains in peaceful activities, whichever is earlier. On that date, the EU and the United States will take the actions described in Sections 20 and 21 of Annex V respectively and Iran will seek, consistent with the Constitutional roles of the President and Parliament, ratification of the Additional Protocol.

v.   UN Security Council resolution Termination Day is the date on which the UN Security Council resolution endorsing this JCPOA terminates according to its terms, which is to be 10 years from Adoption Day, provided that the provisions of previous resolutions have not been reinstated. On that date, the EU will take the actions described in Section 25 of Annex V.

35.   The sequence and milestones set forth above and in Annex V are without prejudice to the duration of JCPOA commitments stated in this JCPOA.

DISPUTE RESOLUTION
MECHANISM

36.   If Iran believed that any or all of the E3/EU+3 were not meeting their
commitments under this JCPOA, Iran could refer the issue to the Joint
Commission for resolution; similarly, if any of the E3/EU+3 believed
that Iran was not meeting its commitments under this JCPOA, any
of the E3/EU+3 could do the same. The Joint Commission would
have 15 days to resolve the issue, unless the time period was extended
by consensus. After Joint Commission consideration, any participant
could refer the issue to Ministers of Foreign Affairs, if it believed the
compliance issue had not been resolved. Ministers would have 15 days
to resolve the issue, unless the time period was extended by consensus.
After Joint Commission consideration – in parallel with (or in lieu of)
review at the Ministerial level - either the complaining participant or
the participant whose performance is in question could request that
the issue be considered by an Advisory Board, which would consist
of three members (one each appointed by the participants in the dispute and a third independent member). The Advisory Board should
provide a non-binding opinion on the compliance issue within 15
days. If, after this 30-day process the issue is not resolved, the Joint
Commission would consider the opinion of the Advisory Board for no
more than 5 days in order to resolve the issue. If the issue still has not
been resolved to the satisfaction of the complaining participant, and

if the complaining participant deems the issue to constitute significant non- performance, then that participant could treat the unresolved issue as grounds to cease performing its commitments under this JCPOA in whole or in part and/or notify the UN Security Council that it believes the issue constitutes significant non-performance. *[This provides an additional unilateral out for Iran.]*

37.   Upon receipt of the notification from the complaining participant, as described above, including a description of the good-faith efforts the participant made to exhaust the dispute resolution process specified in this JCPOA, the UN Security Council, in accordance with its procedures, shall vote on a resolution to continue the sanctions lifting. If the resolution described above has not been adopted within 30 days of the notification, then the provisions of the old UN Security Council resolutions would be re-imposed, unless the UN Security Council decides otherwise. In such event, these provisions would not apply with retroactive effect to contracts signed between any party and Iran or Iranian individuals and entities prior to the date of application, provided that the activities contemplated under and execution of such contracts are consistent with this JCPOA and the previous and current UN Security Council resolutions. The UN Security Council, expressing its intention to prevent the reapplication of the provisions if the issue giving rise to the notification is resolved within this period, intends to take into account the views of the States involved in the issue and any opinion on the issue of the Advisory Board. Iran has stated that if sanctions are reinstated in whole or in part, Iran will treat that as grounds to cease performing its commitments under this JCPOA in whole or in part.

[1]   The provisions of this Resolution do not constitute provisions of this JCPOA. *[What does this mean?]*

[2]   'Government officials' for the U.S. means senior officials of the U.S. Administration.

ANNEX I –
NUCLEAR-RELATED MEASURES

A. *General*

1.   The sequence of implementation of the commitments detailed in this
      Annex is specified in Annex V to the Joint Comprehensive Plan of
      Action (JCPOA). Unless otherwise specified, the durations of the
      commitments in this Annex are from Implementation Day.

B. *Arak Heavy Water Research Reactor*

2.   Iran will modernise the Arak heavy water research reactor to support
      peaceful nuclear research and radioisotopes production for medical
      and industrial purposes. *[The remainder of this provision details the
      means by which this modernization will occur.]*

[…]

C. *Heavy Water Production Plant*

14.   All excess heavy water which is beyond Iran's needs for the modernised
      Arak research reactor, the Zero power heavy water reactor, quantities
      needed for medical research and production of deuterate solutions
      and chemical compounds including, where appropriate, contingency
      stocks, will be made available for export to the international market
      based on international prices and delivered to the international buyer
      for 15 years. Iran's needs, consistent with the parameters above, are
      estimated to be 130 metric tonnes of nuclear grade heavy water or

its equivalent in different enrichments prior to commissioning of the modernised Arak research reactor, and 90 metric tonnes after the commissioning, including the amount contained in the reactor.

15. Iran will inform the IAEA about the inventory and the production of the HWPP and will allow the IAEA to monitor the quantities of the heavy water stocks and the amount of heavy water produced, including through IAEA visits, as requested, to the HWPP.

D. *Other Reactors*

16. Consistent with its plan, Iran will keep pace with the trend of international technological advancement in relying only on light water for its future nuclear power and research reactors with enhanced international cooperation including assurances of supply of necessary fuel.

17. Iran intends to ship out all spent fuel for all future and present nuclear power and research reactors, for further treatment or disposition as provided for in relevant contracts to be concluded consistent with national laws with the recipient party.

E. *Spent Fuel Reprocessing Activities*

18. For 15 years Iran will not, and does not intend to thereafter, engage in any spent fuel reprocessing or spent fuel reprocessing R&D activities. For the purpose of this annex, spent fuel includes all types of irradiated fuel.

19. For 15 years Iran will not, and does not intend to thereafter, reprocess spent fuel except for irradiated enriched uranium targets for production of radio-isotopes for medical and peaceful industrial purposes.

20.   For 15 years Iran will not, and does not intend to thereafter, develop, acquire or build facilities capable of separation of plutonium, uranium or neptunium from spent fuel or from fertile targets, other than for production of radio-isotopes for medical and peaceful industrial purposes.

21.   For 15 years, Iran will only develop, acquire, build, or operate hot cells (containing a cell or interconnected cells), shielded cells or shielded glove boxes with dimensions less than 6 cubic meters in volume compatible with the specifications set out in Annex I of the Additional Protocol. These will be co-located with the modernised Arak research reactor, the Tehran Research Reactor, and radio-medicine production complexes, and only capable of the separation and processing of industrial or medical isotopes and non-destructive PIE. The needed equipment will be acquired through the procurement mechanism established by this JCPOA. For 15 years, Iran will develop, acquire, build, or operate hot cells (containing a cell or interconnected cells), shielded cells or shielded glove boxes with dimensions beyond 6 cubic meters in volume and specifications set out in Annex I of the Additional Protocol, only after approval by the Joint Commission.

22.   The E3/EU+3 are ready to facilitate all of the destructive and non-destructive examinations on fuel elements and/or fuel assembly prototypes including PIE for all fuel fabricated in or outside Iran and irradiated in Iran, using their existing facilities outside Iran. Except for the Arak research reactor complex, Iran will not develop, build, acquire or operate hot cells capable of performing PIE or seek to acquire equipment to build/develop such a capability, for 15 years.

23.   For 15 years, in addition to continuing current fuel testing activities at the TRR, Iran will undertake non-destructive post irradiation examination (PIE) of fuel pins, fuel assembly prototypes and structural materials. These examinations will be exclusively at the Arak research reactor complex. However, the E3/EU+3 will make available their facilities to conduct destructive testing with Iranian specialists, as

agreed. The hot cells at the Arak research reactor in which non-destructive PIE are performed will not be physically interconnected to cells that process or handle materials for the production of medical or industrial radioisotopes.

24. For 15 years, Iran will not engage in producing or acquiring plutonium or uranium metals or their alloys, or conducting R&D on plutonium or uranium (or their alloys) metallurgy, or casting, forming, or machining plutonium or uranium metal.

25. Iran will not produce, seek, or acquire separated plutonium, highly enriched uranium (defined as 20% or greater uranium-235), or uranium-233, or neptunium-237 (except for use as laboratory standards or in instruments using neptunium-237) for 15 years.

26. If Iran seeks to initiate R&D on uranium metal based TRR fuel in small agreed quantities after 10 years and before 15 years, Iran will present its plan to, and seek approval by, the Joint Commission.

F. *Enrichment Capacity*

27. Iran will keep its enrichment capacity at no more than 5060 IR-1 centrifuge machines in no more than 30 cascades in their current configurations in currently operating units at the Natanz Fuel Enrichment Plant (FEP) for 10 years.

28. Iran will keep its level of uranium enrichment at up to 3.67 percent for 15 years.

29. Iran will remove the following excess centrifuges and infrastructure not associated with 5060 IR-1 centrifuges in FEP, which will be stored at Natanz in Hall B of FEP under IAEA continuous monitoring:
[…]

31. For 15 years, Iran will install gas centrifuge machines, or enrichment-related infrastructure, whether suitable for uranium enrichment,

research and development, or stable isotope enrichment, exclusively at the locations and for the activities specified under this JCPOA.

G. *Centrifuges Research and Development*

32.   Iran will continue to conduct enrichment R&D in a manner that does not accumulate enriched uranium. For 10 years and consistent with its enrichment R&D plan, Iran's enrichment R&D with uranium will only include IR-4, IR-5, IR-6 and IR-8 centrifuges.

        […]

35.   Iran will continue the testing of a single IR-4 centrifuge machine and IR-4 centrifuge cascade of up to 10 centrifuge machines for 10 years.

36.   Iran will test a single IR-5 centrifuge machine for 10 years.

        […]

40.   For 15 years, Iran will conduct all testing of centrifuges with uranium only at the PFEP. Iran will conduct all mechanical testing of centrifuges only at the PFEP and the Tehran Research Centre.

H. *Fordow Fuel Enrichment Plant*

44.   The Fordow Fuel Enrichment Plant (FFEP) will be converted into a nuclear, physics, and technology centre and international collaboration will be encouraged in agreed areas of research. The Joint Commission will be informed in advance of the specific projects that will be undertaken at Fordow.

45.   Iran will not conduct any uranium enrichment or any uranium enrichment related R&D and will have no nuclear material at the Fordow Fuel Enrichment Plant (FFEP) for 15 years.

46.   For 15 years, Iran will maintain no more than 1044 IR-1 centrifuge
      machines at one wing of the FFEP of which:

46.   Two cascades that have not experienced UF6 before will be modified
      for the production of stable isotopes. The transition to stable isotope
      production of these cascades at FFEP will be conducted in joint
      partnership between the Russian Federation and Iran on the basis
      of arrangements to be mutually agreed upon. To prepare these two
      cascades for installation of a new cascade architecture appropriate for
      stable isotope production by the joint partnership, Iran will remove
      the connection to the UF6 feed main header, and move cascade UF6
      pipework (except for the dump line in order to maintain vacuum)
      to storage in Fordow under IAEA continuous monitoring. The Joint
      Commission will be informed about the conceptual framework of
      stable isotope production at FFEP. *[This places trust in Russia to
      enforce this provision; see below.]*

      [...]

48.   Iran will:

48.   remove all excess centrifuges and uranium enrichment related infra-
      structure from the other wing of the FFEP. This will include removal
      of all centrifuges and UF6 pipework, including sub headers, valves and
      pressure gauges and transducers, and frequency inverters and convert-
      ers, and UF6 feed and withdrawal stations.

48.   also subsequently remove cascade electrical cabling, individual cas-
      cade control cabinets, vacuum pumps and centrifuge mounting blocks.
      All these excess centrifuges and infrastructure will be stored at Natanz
      in Hall B of FEP under IAEA continuous monitoring.

      [...]

I. *Other Aspects of Enrichment*

52.   Iran will abide by its voluntary commitments as expressed in its own long term enrichment and enrichment R&D plan to be submitted as part of the initial declaration described in Article 2 of the Additional Protocol. The IAEA will confirm on an annual basis, for the duration of the plan that the nature and scope and scale of Iran's enrichment and enrichment R&D activities are in line with this plan.

[...]

J. *Uranium Stocks and Fuels*

56.   Iran will maintain a total enriched uranium stockpile of no more than 300 kg of up to 3.67% enriched uranium hexafluoride (or the equivalent in different chemical forms) for 15 years.

[...]

59.   Russian designed, fabricated and licensed fuel assemblies for use in Russian-supplied reactors in Iran do not count against the 300 kg UF6 stockpile limit.

[...]

K. *Centrifuge Manufacturing*

61.   Consistent with its enrichment and enrichment R&D plan, Iran will only engage in production of centrifuges, including centrifuge rotors suitable for isotope separation or any other centrifuge components, to meet the enrichment and enrichment R&D requirements of this Annex.

[...]

N. *Modern Technologies and Long Term Presence of Iaea*

67.   For the purpose of increasing the efficiency of monitoring for this JCPOA, for 15 years or longer, for the specified verification measures:

67.   Iran will permit the IAEA the use of on-line enrichment measurement and electronic seals which communicate their status within nuclear sites to IAEA inspectors, as well as other IAEA approved and certified modern technologies in line with internationally accepted IAEA practice. Iran will facilitate automated collection of IAEA measurement recordings registered by installed measurement devices and sending to IAEA working space in individual nuclear sites.

67.   Iran will make the necessary arrangements to allow for a long-term IAEA presence, including issuing long-term visas, as well as providing proper working space at nuclear sites and, with best efforts, at locations near nuclear sites in Iran for the designated IAEA inspectors for working and keeping necessary equipment.

67.   Iran will increase the number of designated IAEA inspectors to the range of 130-150 within 9 months from the date of the implementation of the JCPOA, and will generally allow the designation of inspectors from nations that have diplomatic relations with Iran, consistent with its laws and regulations.

O. *Transparency Related to Uranium Ore Concentrate (UOC)*

68.   Iran will permit the IAEA to monitor, through agreed measures that will include containment and surveillance measures, for 25 years, that all uranium ore concentrate produced in Iran or obtained from any other source, is transferred to the uranium conversion facility (UCF)

in Esfahan or to any other future uranium conversion facility which Iran might decide to build in Iran within this period.

69. Iran will provide the IAEA with all necessary information such that the IAEA will be able to verify the production of the uranium ore concentrate and the inventory of uranium ore concentrate produced in Iran or obtained from any other source for 25 years.

P. *Transparency Related to Enrichment*

70. For 15 years, Iran will permit the IAEA to implement continuous monitoring, including through containment and surveillance measures, as necessary, to verify that stored centrifuges and infrastructure remain in storage, and are only used to replace failed or damaged centrifuges, as specified in this Annex.

71. Iran will permit the IAEA regular access, including daily access as requested by the IAEA, to relevant buildings at Natanz, including all parts of the FEP and PFEP, for 15 years.

72. For 15 years, the Natanz enrichment site will be the sole location for all of Iran's uranium enrichment related activities including safeguarded R&D.

73. Iran intends to apply nuclear export policies and practices in line with the internationally established standards for the export of nuclear material, equipment and technology. For 15 years, Iran will only engage, including through export of any enrichment or enrichment related equipment and technology, with any other country, or with any foreign entity in enrichment or enrichment related activities, including related research and development activities, following approval by the Joint Commission.

Q. *Access*

74. Requests for access pursuant to provisions of this JCPOA will be made in good faith, with due observance of the sovereign rights of Iran, and kept to the minimum necessary to effectively implement the verification responsibilities under this JCPOA. *[This provision is extremely vague and allows Iran to invoke its "sovereign rights" to delay or thwart inspection.]* In line with normal international safeguards practice, such requests will not be aimed at interfering with Iranian military or other national security activities, but will be exclusively for resolving concerns regarding fulfilment of the JCPOA commitments and Iran's other non-proliferation and safeguards obligations. The following procedures are for the purpose of JCPOA implementation between the E3/EU+3 and Iran and are without prejudice to the safeguards agreement and the Additional Protocol thereto. In implementing this procedure as well as other transparency measures, the IAEA will be requested to take every precaution to protect commercial, technological and industrial secrets as well as other confidential information coming to its knowledge.

75. In furtherance of implementation of the JCPOA, if the IAEA has concerns regarding undeclared nuclear materials or activities, or activities inconsistent with the JCPOA, at locations that have not been declared under the comprehensive safeguards agreement or Additional Protocol, the IAEA will provide Iran the basis for such concerns and request clarification.

76. If Iran's explanations do not resolve the IAEA's concerns, the Agency may request access to such locations for the sole reason to verify the absence of undeclared nuclear materials and activities or activities inconsistent with the JCPOA at such locations. The IAEA will provide Iran the reasons for access in writing and will make available relevant information.

77. Iran may propose to the IAEA alternative means of resolving the IAEA's concerns that enable the IAEA to verify the absence of undeclared nuclear materials and activities or activities inconsistent with the JCPOA at the location in question, which should be given due and prompt consideration.

78. If the absence of undeclared nuclear materials and activities or activities inconsistent with the JCPOA cannot be verified after the implementation of the alternative arrangements agreed by Iran and the IAEA, or if the two sides are unable to reach satisfactory arrangements to verify the absence of undeclared nuclear materials and activities or activities inconsistent with the JCPOA at the specified locations within 14 days of the IAEA's original request for access, Iran, in consultation with the members of the Joint Commission, would resolve the IAEA's concerns through necessary means agreed between Iran and the IAEA. In the absence of an agreement, the members of the Joint Commission, by consensus or by a vote of 5 or more of its 8 members, would advise on the necessary means to resolve the IAEA's concerns. The process of consultation with, and any action by, the members of the Joint Commission would not exceed 7 days, and Iran would implement the necessary means within 3 additional days. *[This is a dangerous provision that may allow Iran to remove, destroy, or relocate incriminating material during the overly long access process.]*

R. *Centrifuge Component Manufacturing Transparency*

79. Iran and the IAEA will take the necessary steps for containment and surveillance on centrifuge rotor tubes and bellows for 20 years.

80. In this context:

80. Iran will provide the IAEA with an initial inventory of all existing centrifuge rotor tubes and bellows and subsequent reports on changes in

such inventory and will permit the IAEA to verify the inventory by item counting and numbering, and through containment and surveillance, of all rotor tubes and bellows, including in all existing and newly produced centrifuges.

80.   Iran will declare all locations and equipment, namely flow-forming machines, filament- winding machines and mandrels that are used for production of centrifuge rotor tubes or bellows, and will permit the IAEA to implement continuous monitoring, including through containment and surveillance on this equipment, to verify that this equipment is being used to manufacture centrifuges only for the activities specified in this JCPOA.

S.   *Other Uranium Isotope Separation Activities*

81.   For 10 years, Iran's uranium isotope separation-related research and development or production activities will be exclusively based on gaseous centrifuge technology. Iran will permit IAEA access to verify that uranium isotope separation production and R&D activities are consistent with this Annex.

T.   *Activities Which Could Contribute to the Design and Development of a Nuclear Explosive Device*

82.   Iran will not engage in the following activities which could contribute to the development of a nuclear explosive device:

82.   Designing, developing, acquiring, or using computer models to simulate nuclear explosive devices.

82.   Designing, developing, fabricating, acquiring, or using multi-point explosive detonation systems suitable for a nuclear explosive device,

unless approved by the Joint Commission for non-nuclear purposes and subject to monitoring.

82.   Designing, developing, fabricating, acquiring, or using explosive diagnostic systems (streak cameras, framing cameras and flash x-ray cameras) suitable for the development of a nuclear explosive device, unless approved by the Joint Commission for non-nuclear purposes and subject to monitoring.

82.   Designing, developing, fabricating, acquiring, or using explosively driven neutron sources or specialized materials for explosively driven neutron sources. *[This is a good provision if it is properly enforced.]*

[...]

ANNEX II –
SANCTIONS-RELATED
COMMITMENTS

[...]

A. *European Union*

1. The EU and EU Member States commit to terminate all provisions of Council Regulation (EU) No 267/2012 (as subsequently amended) implementing all nuclear-related sanctions or restrictive measures as specified in Sections 1.1-1.10 below, to terminate all provisions of Council Decision 2010/413/CFSP (as subsequently amended), as specified in Sections 1.1-1.10 below, and to terminate or amend national implementing legislation as required, in accordance with Annex V:

1. Financial, banking and insurance measures *[This details such measures as specified in the agreement.]*

   [...]

1. Oil, gas and petrochemical sectors

   [...]

1. Shipping, shipbuilding and transport sectors

[…]

1.   Gold, other precious metals, banknotes and coinage

      [...]

1.   Nuclear proliferation-related measures

      [...]

1.   Metals

1.   Sanctions on metals (Articles 4e and 4f of Council Decision 2010/413/CFSP; Articles 15a, 15b and 15c, and Annex VIIB of Council Regulation (EU) No 267/2012); and

1.   Sanctions on associated services for the category above (see the references above).

1.   Software

      [...]

1.   Arms

      [...]

1.   Listing of persons, entities and bodies (asset freeze and visa ban)

      [...]

3.   Effects of the lifting of EU economic and financial sanctions

3.   As a result of the lifting of sanctions specified in Section 1 above, the following activities, including associated services, will be allowed, beginning on implementation day, in accordance with this JCPOA and provided that such activities are otherwise consistent with EU and EU Member States' laws and regulations in effect:

3.   Financial, banking and insurance measures (See Sections 1.1.1 to 1.1.8)

      [...]

3.   Oil, gas and petrochemical sectors (See Sections 1.2.1 to 1.2.5)

      [...]

3.   Shipping, shipbuilding and transport sectors (See Sections 1.3.1 to 1.3.3)

      [...]

3.   Gold, other precious metals, banknotes and coinage (See Sections 1.4.1 to 1.4.2)

      [...]

3.   Metals (See Sections 1.6.1 to 1.6.2)

      [...]

3.   Software (See Sections 1.7.1 to 1.7.2)

      [...]

3.   Listing of persons, entities and bodies (asset freeze and visa ban) (See Section 1.9.1)

      [...]

B. *United States*

4.   The United States commits to cease the application of, and to seek such legislative action as may be appropriate to terminate, or modify to effectuate the termination of, all nuclear-related sanctions as specified in Sections 4.1-4.9 below, and to terminate Executive Orders 13574, 13590, 13622 and 13645, and Sections 5-7 and 15 of Executive Order 13628, in accordance with Annex V.

4.1. Financial and banking measures

      [...]

4.2. Insurance measures

      [...]

4.3. Energy and petrochemical sectors

      [...]

4.4. Shipping, shipbuilding and port sectors

      [...]

4.5. Gold and other precious metals

      [...]

4.6. Software and metals

[...]

4.7.   Automotive sector

        [...]

4.8.   Designations and other sanctions listings

        [...]

4.9.   Nuclear proliferation-related measures

4.9.1. Sanctions under the Iran, North Korea and Syria Nonproliferation
        Act on the acquisition of nuclear-related commodities and services for
        nuclear activities contemplated in the JCPOA, to be consistent with
        the U.S. approach to other non-nuclear-weapon states under the NPT;

1.   Sanctions on joint ventures relating to the mining, production, or
        transportation of uranium (ISA Section 5(b)(2)); and

1.   Exclusion of Iranian citizens from higher education coursework related
        to careers in nuclear science, nuclear engineering or the energy sector
        (TRA Section 501).

5.   Other trade measures

5.1.   The United States commits to:

5.1.1. Allow for the sale of commercial passenger aircraft and related parts
        and services to Iran by licensing the (i) export, re-export, sale, lease
        or transfer to Iran of commercial passenger aircraft for exclusively civil
        aviation end-use, (ii) export, re-export, sale, lease or transfer to Iran
        of spare parts and components for commercial passenger aircraft, and
        (iii) provision of associated serviced, including warranty, maintenance,
        and repair services and safety-related inspections, for all the forego-
        ing, provided that licensed items and services are used exclusively for
        commercial passenger aviation;

5.1.2. License non-U.S. entities that are owned or controlled by a U.S. person
        to engage in activities with Iran that are consistent with this JCPOA;
        and

5.1.3. License the importation into the United States of Iranian-origin car-
        pets and foodstuffs, including pistachios and caviar.

6.   The United States represents that the provisions listed in Section 4
      above constitute the full and complete list of all U.S. nuclear-related
      sanctions. These sanctions will be lifted in accordance with Annex V.
      […]

7.   Financial and banking measures (See Sections 4.1.1 to 4.1.7)
      […]

7.   Insurance measures (See Section 4.2.1)
      […]

7.   Energy and petrochemical sectors (See Sections 4.3.1 to 4.3.6)
      […]

7.   Shipping, shipbuilding and port sectors (See Sections 4.4.1 to 4.4.2)
      […]

7.   Gold and other precious metals (See Sections 4.5.1 to 4.5.2)
      […]

7.   Software and metals (See Sections 4.6.1 to 4.6.2)
      […]

7.   Automotive sector (See Sections 4.7.1 to 4.7.2)
      […]

7.   Designations and other sanctions listings (See Section 4.8.1)
      […]

ANNEX III - CIVIL NUCLEAR COOPERATION

A. General

1. Iran and E3/ EU+3 decided to co-operate, among others, including through IAEA technical cooperation, where appropriate, and without prejudice to existing bilateral agreements, in different areas of civil nuclear co-operation to be developed with the frameworks of this JCPOA, as detailed in this Annex. In this context, the Joint Commission will also support assistance to Iran, including through IAEA technical cooperation projects as appropriate.

    […]

10. Nuclear Security

     [The below provisions have been interpreted by some commentators as imposing an obligation on the United States and its negotiating partners to help prevent sabotage to Iran's nuclear infrastructure. The language does not appear obligatory, but nevertheless, Congress should inquire as to the purpose of including "anti-sabotage" as an area of possible cooperation between the signatory parties.]

     E3/EU+3 parties, and possibly other states, as appropriate, are prepared to cooperate with Iran on the implementation of nuclear security guidelines and best practices. Co-operation in the following areas can be envisaged:

10. Co-operation in the form of training courses and workshops to strengthen Iran's ability to prevent, protect and respond to nuclear security threats to nuclear facilities and systems as well as to enable effective and sustainable nuclear security and physical protection systems;

10. Co-operation through training and workshops to strengthen Iran's ability to protect against, and respond to nuclear security threats, including sabotage, as well as to enable effective and sustainable nuclear security and physical protection systems.

[…]

ANNEX IV –
JOINT COMMISSION

1. *Establishment, Composition, and Coordinator*

1. The Joint Commission is established to carry out the functions assigned to it in the JCPOA, including its Annexes.

1. The Joint Commission is comprised of representatives of Iran and the E3/EU+3 (China, France, Germany, the Russian Federation, the United Kingdom, and the United States, with the High Representative of the Union for Foreign Affairs and Security Policy), together, the JCPOA participants.

1. The Joint Commission may establish Working Groups in particular areas, as appropriate.

1. The High Representative of the Union for Foreign Affairs and Security Policy ('High Representative'), or his/her designated representative will serve as the Coordinator of the Joint Commission.

2. *Functions*

2. The Joint Commission will perform the following functions:

1.   Review and approve the final design for the modernized heavy water research reactor and the design of the subsidiary laboratories prior to the commencement of construction, and review and approve the fuel design for the modernized heavy water research reactor as provided for in Section B of Annex I;

2.   Review and approve, upon request by Iran, development, acquisition, construction or operation of hot cells (containing a cell or interconnected cells), shielded cells or shielded glove boxes with dimensions beyond 6 cubic meters in volume and specifications set out in Annex I of the Additional Protocol, as provided for in paragraph 21 of Annex I;

3.   Review and approve plans submitted by Iran to initiate R&D on uranium metal based TRR fuel, as provided for in paragraph 26 of Annex I;

4.   Review and approve, upon request by Iran, projects on new types of centrifuges to proceed to a prototype stage for mechanical testing, as provided for in paragraph 43 of Annex I;

5.   Receive information in advance about the specific projects that will be undertaken at Fordow, as provided for in paragraph 44 of Annex I;

6.   Receive information about the conceptual framework of stable isotope production at Fordow, as provided for in paragraph 46.1 of Annex I;

1.   Assess and then approve, upon request by Iran, that fuel assemblies manufactured in Iran and their intermediate products cannot be readily reconverted into UF6, based on the objective technical criteria, with the goal of enabling fuel to be fabricated in Iran, as provided in paragraph 59 of Annex I;

2.   Support assistance to Iran, including through IAEA technical cooperation as appropriate, in meeting international qualification standards for nuclear fuel produced by Iran, as provided for in paragraph 59 of Annex I;

3. Review and approve in advance, upon request by Iran, engagement by Iran, including through export of any enrichment or enrichment related equipment and technology, with any other country, or with any foreign entity in enrichment and enrichment related activities, including related research and development, as provided for in paragraph 73 in Annex I;

4. Provide consultation, and advise on the necessary means in the context of access as specified in paragraph 78 of Annex I;

5. Review and approve in advance, upon request by Iran, the design, development, fabrication, acquisition, or use for non-nuclear purposes of multi-point explosive detonation systems suitable for a nuclear explosive device and explosive diagnostic systems (streak cameras, framing cameras and flash x-ray cameras) suitable for the development of a nuclear explosive device, as provided for in paragraphs 82.2 and 82.3 of Annex I;

6. Review and consult to address issues arising from the implementation of sanctions lifting as specified in this JCPOA and its Annex II;

7. Review and decide on proposals for nuclear-related transfers to or activities with, Iran, in accordance with Section 6 of this Annex and the United Nations Security Council resolution endorsing this JCPOA;

8. Review, with a view to resolving, any issue that a JCPOA participant believes constitutes nonperformance by another JCPOA participant of its commitments under the JCPOA, according to the process outlined in the JCPOA;

9. Adopt or modify, as necessary, procedures to govern its activities;

10. Consult and provide guidance on other implementation matters that may arise under the JCPOA.

    […]

4. *Decisions*

4. Except as stated otherwise in this Annex, decisions by the Joint Commission are to be made by consensus.

4. Each JCPOA participant will have one vote. Decisions of the Joint Commission are to be taken by the Representative or the Deputy Representative or other such alternate as the JCPOA participant may designate.

4. The vote of each JCPOA participant will be made known to all other JCPOA participants if any JCPOA participant requests a recorded vote.

4. Matters before the Joint Commission pursuant to Section Q of Annex I are to be decided by consensus or by affirmative vote of five JCPOA participants. There is no quorum requirement.

[...]

ANNEX V -
IMPLEMENTATION PLAN

1. This Annex describes the sequence of the actions specified in Annexes I and II to this JCPOA.

A. *Finalisation Day*

2. Upon conclusion of the negotiations of this JCPOA, the E3/EU+3 (China, France, Germany, the Russian Federation, the United Kingdom and the United States, with the High Representative of the European Union for Foreign Affairs and Security Policy) and Iran will endorse this JCPOA.

3. Promptly after the conclusion of the negotiations of this JCPOA, the proposed UN Security Council resolution referred to in Section 18 of this Annex will be submitted to the UN Security Council for adoption without delay.

4. The EU will promptly endorse the UN Security Council resolution referred to above through Council Conclusions.

5. Iran and the IAEA will start developing necessary arrangements to implement all transparency measures provided for in this JCPOA so that such arrangements are completed, in place, and ready for implementation on Implementation Day.

B. *Adoption Day*

6. Adoption Day will occur 90 days after the endorsement of this JCPOA by the UN Security Council through the resolution referred to above, or at an earlier date by mutual consent of all JCPOA participants, at which point this JCPOA comes into effect.

7. Beginning on Adoption Day, JCPOA participants will make necessary arrangements and preparations, including legal and administrative preparations, for the implementation of their JCPOA commitments.

8. Iran will officially inform the IAEA that, effective on Implementation Day, Iran will provisionally apply the Additional Protocol, pending its ratification by the Majlis (Parliament), and will fully implement the modified code 3.1.

9. Iran will implement paragraph 66 from Section M on "Past and Present Issues of Concern" of Annex I.

10. The EU and its Member States will adopt an EU Regulation, taking effect as of Implementation Day, terminating all provisions of the EU Regulation implementing all nuclear-related economic and financial EU sanctions as specified in Section 16.1 of this Annex, simultaneously with the IAEA-verified implementation by Iran of agreed nuclear-related measures.

11. The United States, acting pursuant to Presidential authorities, will issue waivers, to take effect upon Implementation Day, ceasing the application of the statutory nuclear-related sanctions as specified in Sections 17.1 to 17.2 of this Annex. The President will also take action to direct that all appropriate additional measures be taken to implement the cessation of application of sanctions as specified in Sections 17.1 to 17.4 of this Annex, including the termination of Executive orders as specified in Section 17.4, and the licensing of activities as specified in Section 17.5.

12.   E3/EU+3 participants and Iran will begin discussions on an official
       document to be concluded in advance of Implementation Day which
       will express strong commitments of the E3/EU+3 participants to
       the Arak Heavy Water Reactor modernisation project and define the
       responsibilities assumed by the E3/EU+3 participants.

13.   The EU, its Member States and the United States will begin consulta-
       tion as appropriate with Iran regarding relevant guidelines and publicly
       accessible statements on the details of sanctions or restrictive mea-
       sures to be lifted under this JCPOA.

c. *Implementation Day*

14.   Implementation Day will occur upon the IAEA-verified implementa-
       tion by Iran of the nuclear-related measures described in paragraph 15
       below, and, simultaneously, the E3/EU+3 taking the actions described
       in paragraphs 16 and 17 below, and with the actions described in para-
       graph 18 below taking place at the UN level in accordance with the
       UN Security Council resolution.

**15.   Iran will implement the nuclear-related measures as specified in
       Annex I:**
       [...]

16.   The European Union will: *[Cease the application of sanctions.]*
       [...]

17.   The United States will:

17.   Cease the application of the sanctions set forth in Sections 4.1 - 4.5
       and 4.7 of Annex II, with the exception of Section 211(a) of the Iran
       Threat Reduction and Syria Human Rights Act of 2012 (TRA);

17.   Cease the application of the sanctions set forth in Section 4.6 of Annex
       II, in connection with activities consistent with this JCPOA, including

trade with individuals and entities set forth in Attachment 3 to Annex II;

17. Remove individuals and entities set forth in Attachment 3 to Annex II from the Specially Designated Nationals and Blocked Persons List (SDN List), the Foreign Sanctions Evaders List (FSE List), and/or the Non-SDN Iran Sanctions Act List as set forth in Section 4.8.1 of Annex II;

17. Terminate Executive Orders 13574, 13590, 13622, 13645 and Sections 5-7 and 15 of Executive Order 13628 as set forth in Section 4 of Annex II; and

17. License activities as set forth in Section 5 of Annex II.

18.   UN Security Council

18. In accordance with the UN Security Council resolution endorsing this JCPOA, the provisions imposed in UN Security Council resolutions 1696 (2006), 1737 (2006), 1747 (2007), 1803 (2008), 1835 (2008), 1929 (2010) and 2224 (2015) will be terminated subject to re-imposition in the event of significant non-performance by Iran of JCPOA commitments, and specific restrictions, including restrictions regarding the transfer of proliferation sensitive goods will apply.

18. The E3/EU+3 will take appropriate measures to implement the new UNSC resolution.

D. *Transition Day*

19. Transition Day will occur 8 years from Adoption Day or upon a report from the Director General of the IAEA to the IAEA Board of Governors and in parallel to the UN Security Council stating that the IAEA has reached the Broader Conclusion that all nuclear material in Iran remains in peaceful activities, whichever is earlier.

20.   The European Union will:

20. Terminate the provisions of Council Regulation (EU) No 267/2012 and suspend the corresponding provisions of Council Decision 2010/413/CFSP specified in Sections 1.1.4, 1.3.2 (in so far as it concerns Articles 15 and 18 of Council Decision and Articles 36 and 37 of Council Regulation); 1.5.1 and 1.5.2 (in so far as it concerns Ballistic Missiles restrictions); 1.6.1 - 1.9.1 of Annex II.

[...]

21. The United States will:

21. Seek such legislative action as may be appropriate to terminate, or modify to effectuate the termination of, the statutory sanctions set forth in Sections 4.1-4.5, 4.7 and 4.9 of Annex II;

21. Seek such legislative action as may be appropriate to terminate, or modify to effectuate the termination of, the statutory sanctions described in Section 4.6 of Annex II, in connection with activities consistent with this JCPOA, including trade with individuals and entities set forth in Attachments 3 and 4 to Annex II; and

21. Remove individuals and entities set out in Attachment 4 to Annex II from the SDN List and/or the FSE List as set forth in Section 4.8.1 of Annex II.

22. Iran will:

22. Seek, consistent with the Constitutional roles of the President and Parliament, ratification of the Additional Protocol.

E. *UNSCR Termination Day*

23. UNSCR (UN Security Council resolution) Termination Day will occur in accordance with the terms of the UN Security Council resolution endorsing the JCPOA, which is 10 years from Adoption Day, provided that the provisions of previous resolutions have not been reinstated.

24. On UNSCR Termination Day, the provisions and measures imposed in that resolution would terminate and the UN Security Council would no longer be seized of the Iran nuclear issue.

25. The European Union will:

25. Terminate all remaining provisions of Council Regulation (EU) No 267/2012 and Council Decision 2010/413/CFSP.

F. *Other*

26. The terminations described in this Annex V are without prejudice to other JCPOA commitments that would continue beyond such termination dates.

NOTES

1. Suzanne Fields, "Confronting the New Anti-Semitism," *The Washington Times*, 25 July 2004

2. Ibid.

3. Greg Bruno, "Iran's Ballistic Missile Program," *The Council on Foreign Relations Background Paper*, 23 July 2012

4. Jeffrey Goldberg, "Obama's Crystal-Clear Promises to Stop Iran from Getting a Nuclear Weapon," *The Atlantic*, 2 October 2012

5. Abraham C. Weinfeld, "What did the Framers of the Federal Constitution Mean by 'Agreements or Compacts?'" *The University of Chicago Law Review*, (1935–1936), pp. 453–64

6. Gernot Heller, "Germany Says Iran Must Improve Israel Relations for Closer Economic Ties," *Reuters*, 19 July 2015

7. "Iran reaffirms that under no circumstances will Iran ever seek, develop, or acquire any nuclear weapons." *Joint Comprehensive Plan of Action*, Vienna, 14 July 2015

7. See Olivier Corten and Pierre Klein, *The Vienna Conventions on the Law of Treaties: A Commentary*, Oxford University Press, New York: 2011, p.6

8. See for example "Obama: Lifting of Sanctions Will Increase Iran's Ability to Finance Terrorists," *Jerusalem Post*, 24 July 2015

9. Full Text: "Obama: 'It Would Be Irresponsible to Walk Away From' Iran Nuclear Deal," *Washington Post*, 14 July 2015

10. "Transcript: President Obama's Full NPR Interview on Iran Nuclear Deal," NPR, 7 April 2015

11. Terry Atlas, "Obama's Own Words Lead to Confusion Over Iran Nuclear Timeline," *Bloomberg Politics*, 8 April 2015

12. See David E. Sanger and Michael R. Gordon, "Years of Trading and Compromise Sealed Iran Deal," *New York Times*, 16 July 2015 (emphasis added)

13. Thomas L. Friedman, "Obama Makes His Case on Iran Nuclear Deal," *New York Times*, 14 July 2015 (emphasis added)

14. Ibid.

15. Tamar Pileggi, "Obama: There Is No Military Option to Stop Iran," *Times of Israel*, 1 June 2015

16. Ibid.

17. David E. Sanger and Michael R. Gordon, "Clearing Hurdles to Iran Nuclear Deal with Standoffs, Shouts and Compromise," *New York Times*, 15 July 2015

18. See for example Tamar Pileggi, "Obama: There Is No Military Option to Stop Iran," *Times of Israel*, 1 June 2015

19. Thomas L. Friedman, "Backing up Our Wager with Iran," *New York Times*, 22 July 2015

20. See Part 4, Section B of this book

21. Jeffrey Goldberg, "Obama's Crystal-Clear Promise to Stop Iran from Getting a Nuclear Weapon," *The Atlantic*, 2 October 2012

22. Ibid.

23. Ibid.

24. Jeffrey Goldberg, "Obama's Crystal-Clear Promise to Stop Iran from Getting a Nuclear Weapon," *The Atlantic*, 2 October 2012

25. "Obama Intimates US to Strike Iran in a Year if Diplomacy Fails: US president, in interview with Channel 2, says that 'If we can resolve it diplomatically, that's a more lasting solution,'" *Times of Israel*, 14 March 2013

26. Chelsea J. Carter, "Obama: Iran More than a Year Away from Developing Nuclear Weapons," CNN, 15 March 2013

27. Julian Borger, "Barack Obama Warns Iran that US is Still Prepared to Take Military Action," *The Guardian*, 15 September 2013

28. "US President Says Iran 'A Year or More Away from a Nuclear Bomb,' and American Assessments 'More Conservative' than the Israelis," *Associated Press*, 5 October 2013

29. "Statement by the President on First Step Agreement on Iran's Nuclear Program," White House Office of the Press Secretary, 23 November 2013

30. Conor Finnegan, "Obama Defends Iran Deal," CNN, 7 December 2013

31. Jeffrey Goldberg, "Obama to Israel—Time Is Running Out," *Bloomberg*, 2 March 2014

32. "Face the Nation Transcripts November 9, 2014: Obama, Bush," CBS News, 9 November 2014

33. Brian Knowlton, "Obama Acknowledge Broad Gaps between 2 Sides in Iran Nuclear Talk," *New York Times*, 23 November 2014

34. "Transcript: President Obama's Full NPR Interview," National Public Library, 29 December 2014

35. Jeff Mason, "Exclusive: Obama Says Iran Must Halt Key Nuclear Work for at Least a Decade," *Reuters*, 2 March 2015

36. "Transcript: President Obama's Full NPR Interview on Iran Nuclear Deal," National Public Radio, 7 April 2015

37. Barak Ravid, "Obama: Only a Deal Will Stop Iran Having Nukes, Attack Won't Help," *Haaretz*, 1 June 2015

38. Thomas L. Friedman, "Obama Makes His Case on Iran Nuclear Deal," *New York Times*, 14 July 2015

39. "Leader Rejects Continued N. Talks Under Threat," *Fars News Agency*, 6 May 2015

40. "Former Shin Bet Chief: Iran Deal Is Best Option for Israel," *Jerusalem Post*, 21 July 2015

41. "Russia to Supply Iran with Missile Defense System," *Al-Jazeera Politics Online*, 14 April 2015

42. "Joint Comprehensive Plan of Action," Vienna, 14 July 2015, retrieved via "Full Text of the Iran Nuclear Deal," *Washington Post*, 14 July 2015

43. "Kerry: Israeli Action Against Iran Would Be a Huge Mistake," *Reuters*, 24 July 2015

44. Thomas L. Friedman, "Obama Makes His Case on Iran Nuclear Deal," *New York Times*, 14 July 2015

45. David E. Sanger, "Obama's Leap of Faith on Iran," *New York Times*, 14 July 2015.

46. Reena Flores, "Obama Fires Back at 'Dishonest' Iran Deal Critics," CBS News, 18 July 2015

47. Alan Dershowitz, *Preemption: A Knife that Cuts Both Ways (Issues of Our Time),*" (New York: W.W. Norton & Co., 2007)

48. Steven Stalinsky, "Iranian Talk of an Attack on America," *New York Sun*, 18 August 2004

49. Jerome R. Corsi, *Atomic Iran: How the Terrorist Regime Bought the Bomb and American Politicians,*(Nashville: WND Books, 2005), p. 42

50. Craig S. Smith, "Iran Moves Towards Enriching Uranium," *New York Times*, 22 September 2004, and Ali Akbar Dareini, "Iranian Lawmakers, Shouting 'Death to America,' Vote Unanimously for Resuming Uranium Enrichment," *Associated Press*, 31 October 2004

51. "Iran Confirms Processing Tons of Uranium Ore," *New York Times*, 10 May 2005

52. Tom Hundley, "Blair Warns Iran He May Seek Sanctions on Nuclear Plans," *Chicago Tribune*, 13 May 2005

53. Tom Hundley, "Pressure Builds on Iran; Blair Says UN Security Council Is Next Stop if Nuclear Work Resumes," *Chicago Tribune*, 13 May 2005

54. Seymour M. Hersh, "The Coming Wars," *New Yorker*, 24 and 31 January 2005

55. Ibid.

56. David E. Sanger, "Rice Says Iran Must Not Be Allowed to Develop Nuclear Arms," *New York Times*, 9 August 2004, p. A3

57. See for example Anton La Guardia, "Israel Challenges Iran's Nuclear Ambitions," *Daily Telegraph*, 22 September 2004

58. Corsi, op. cit., p.32

59. Quoted in Hersh, op. cit., p.44

60. Quoted in H.D.S. Greenway, "Onward to Iran?" *Boston Globe*, 4 February 2005, p.A15

61. See Geneva Conventions of 12 August 1949, and relating to the Protection of Victims of International Armed Conflicts, 8 June 1977, Part IV, Section I, Chapter I, Article 48

62. Arieh O'Sullivan, "Ya'alon: We Must Be Prepared to Strike Iran," *Jerusalem Post*, 14 December 2004

63. Corsi, op. cit., p. 32

64. Hersh, "The Coming Wars," loc. cit.

65. Hersh, "The Coming Wars," loc. cit.

66. Hersh, "The Coming Wars," loc. cit.

67. Steven R. Weisman, "Bush Aides Divided on Confronting Iran Over A-Bomb," *New York Times*, 21 September 2004

68. Matthew Continetti, "International Men of Mystery," *Weekly Standard*, 21 October 2004

69. See p. 44 infra

70. Alan Dershowitz, "We Can't Attack Iran," *The Spectator*, 22 April 2006

71. Alan Dershowitz, "Why I Support Israel and Obama," *Huffington Post*, 11 November 2008

72. Alan Dershowitz, "Don't Blame Israel," *New York Post*, 9 May 2009

73. Alan Dershowitz, "Obama's Legacy and the Iranian Bomb: Neville Chamberlain was remembered for appeasing Germany, not his progressive social programs," *Wall Street Journal*, 23 March 2010

74. Alan Dershowitz, "The Obama Administration's Conflicting Messages on Iran," *Huffington Post*, 19 June 2010

75. See David E. Sanger and Thom Shanker, "Gates Says US Lacks a Policy to Thwart Iran," *New York Times*, 17 April 2010

76. Alan Dershowitz, "There Will Never be Peace if Iran Gets the Bomb," *Jerusalem Post*, 1 December 2010

77. See for example Ian Black and Simon Tisdall, "Saudi Arabia Urges US Attack on Iran to Stop Nuclear Programme," *The Guardian*, 28 November 2010

78. See "US Report: Iran Stopped Nuclear Weapons Work in 2003," CNN, 3 December 2007

79. Alan Dershowitz, "Obama, Israel & American Jews: The Challenge," *Commentary Magazine*, 1 June 2010

80. David E. Sanger and Thom Shanker, "Gates Says US Lacks a Policy to Thwart Iran," *New York Times*, 17 April 2010

81. Alan Dershowitz, "WikiLeaks Cables: The Middle East Fallout Could be Grave," *The Guardian*, 2 December 2010

82. "US Report: Iran Stopped Nuclear Weapons Work in 2003," CNN, 3 December 2007

83. Alan Dershowitz, "Israel and the US: Behind the Tension—Is Friendship a One-Way Street?" *New York Daily News*, 4 February 2011

84. Alan Dershowitz, "Israel Has the Right to Attack Iran's Nuclear Reactors Now," *Huffington Post*, 16 March 2011

85. Yonat Frilling, "50 Tons of Smuggled Weapons Seized," *Fox News*, 16 March 2011

86. Edmund Sanders, "Brutal West Bank Killings Shock Israel, Stir Fears of Renewed Violence," *Los Angeles Times*, 13 March 2011

87. Alan Dershowitz, "WikiLeaks Contradicts Obama Administration on Iran," *Huffington Post*, 25 May 2011

88. See Ian Black and Simon Tisdall, "Saudi Arabia Urges US Attack on Iran to Stop Nuclear Programme," *The Guardian*, 28 November 2010 or David E. Sanger, James Glanz, and Jo Becker, "Around the World, Distress Over Iran," *New York Times*, 28 November 2010

89. Chas Freeman, "Why Iran Loves WikiLeaks," *New York Times*, 4 December 2010

90. Alan Dershowitz, "President Obama has Right Goals on Israeli-Palestinian Peace, but Strategy Already Backfiring," *New York Daily News*, 27 May 2011

91. "Remarks by the President on the Middle East and North Africa," White House Office of the Press Secretary, 19 May 2011

92. Alan Dershowitz, "Warning Iran Against Hitting 'Soft' American Targets," *Wall Street Journal*, 13 February 2012

93. Alan Dershowitz, "President Obama Turns a Corner on Iran," *The Gatestone Institute*, 2 March 2012

94. Jeffrey Goldberg, "Obama to Iran and Israel: 'As President of the United States, I Don't Bluff,'" *The Atlantic*, 2 March 2012

95. Alan Dershowitz, "Assessing President Obama's Trip," *Huffington Post*, 22 March 2013

96. William J. Broad, "Weapons Experts Raise Doubts About Israel's Antimissile System," *New York Times*, 20 March 2013

97. Alan Dershowitz, "J Street Undercuts Obama's Policy on Iran," *Jerusalem Post*, 14 June 2012

98. See http://jstreet.org/page/mythsandfacts/our-policies - myth_3

99. "Dagan Defends Discourse on Iranian Threat," *The Jerusalem Post*, 10 June 2012

100. Alan Dershowitz, "President Obama can Stop Iran," *Newsmax*, 31 August 2012

101. Alan Dershowitz, "The Message Obama Should Have Sent," *Wall Street Journal*, 26 September 2012

102. Louis Charbonneau, "In New York, Defiant Ahmadinejad Says Israel Will Be Eliminated," *Reuters*, 24 September 2012

103. Alan Dershowitz, "President's Nomination of Hagel May Encourage Iran's Nuclear Ambition," The Gatestone Institute, 7 January 2013 or *Huffington Post* under same title and date

104. Alan Dershowitz, "Obama: Get Approval from Congress on Iran Now," *Haaretz*, 5 September 2013

105. Alan Dershowitz, "How the New York Times Distorted Netanyahu's UN Speech," *Haaretz*, 2 October 2013

106. Alan Dershowitz, "Oppose the Deal on Iran," *Haaretz*, 12 November 2013

107. Alan Dershowitz, "Congress Must Keep the Military Option on the Table," *Haaretz*, 27 November 2013

108. Alan Dershowitz, "The Education of a Wartime President," *Wall Street Journal*, 5 October 2014

109. Alan Dershowitz, "Why is the Obama Administration Provoking Israel?" *Jerusalem Post*, 6 November 2014

110. Jeffrey Goldberg, "The Crisis in U.S.-Israel Relations Is Officially Here," *The Atlantic*, 28 October 2014

111. Alan Dershowitz, "Will the New Congress Push Obama into Being Tougher on Iran's Nuclear Weapons Program?" *The Hill*, 11 November 2014

112. "Report: Alan Dershowitz Convinced Rep Rangel to Attend Netanyahu Congress Speech," *The Algemeiner*, 20 May 2015

113. Alan Dershowitz, "The Appalling Talk of Boycotting Netanyahu," *Wall Street Journal*, 23 February 2015

114. Alan Dershowitz, "White House Must Respond to Netanyahu's Important New Proposal," *Jerusalem Post*, 4 March 2015

115. Alan Dershowitz, "Supporters of Deal Are Strengthening Iran's Negotiating Position," *Jerusalem Post*, 10 March 2015

116. Alan Dershowitz, "President Is Not Commander in Chief of Foreign Policy," *The Gatestone Institute*, 17 March 2015

117. Alan Dershowitz, "Obama Is Neither Anti-Israel nor Anti-Semitic," *Jerusalem Post*, 22 May 2015

118. Alan Dershowitz, "Does This Deal Prevent Iran from Developing a Nuclear Weapon?" *Jerusalem Post*, 15 July 2015

119. "Transcript: President Obama's Full NPR Interview on Iran Nuclear Deal," National Public Radio, 7 April 2015

120. "Statement by the President on Iran," White House Office of the Press Secretary, 14 July 2015

121. William J. Clinton, "Remarks on the Nuclear Agreement with North Korea," 18 October 1994

122. Alan Dershowitz, "US Gave Away Better Options on Iran," *Boston Globe*, 16 July 2015

123. David D. Kirkpatrick and Ben Hubbard, "King Salman of Saudi Arabia Meets with Hamas Leaders," *New York Times*, 18 July 2015, p. A5.

124. See Thomas Erdbrink, "Ayatollah Khamenei, Backing Iran Negotiators, Endorses Nuclear Deal," *New York Times*, 18 July 2015

125. "Leader Rejects Continued N. Talks Under Threat," *Fars News Agency*, 6 May 2015

126. "Kerry's Threats and Intimidation Won't Silence Israel, Officials Tell NYT," *Times of Israel*, 26 July 2015

127. Thomas L. Friedman, "Backing up Our Wager with Iran," *New York Times*, 22 July 2015

128. Jeffrey Goldberg, "Obama's Crystal-Clear Promise to Stop Iran from Getting a Nuclear Weapon," *The Atlantic*, 2 October 2012

129. Jonathan S. Tobin, "Obama Lobby Smear in Iran Deal Debate Cannot Go Unanswered," *Commentary Magazine*, 22 July 2015

130. "Iran reaffirms that under no circumstances will Iran ever seek, develop, or acquire any nuclear weapons." *Joint Comprehensive Plan of Action*, Vienna, 14 July 2015

131. The material in this timeline was compiled with reference to the following helpful sources: Ariana Rowberry, "Sixty Years of 'Atoms for Peace' and Iran's Nuclear Program," *The Brookings Institution*, 18 December 2013; Shreeya Sinha and Susan Campbell Beachy, "Timeline of Iran's Nuclear Program," *New York Times*, 2 April 2015; and Kate Lyons, "Iran Nuclear Talks: Timeline," *The Guardian*, 14 July 2015

CPSIA information can be obtained
at www.ICGtesting.com
Printed in the USA
FSOW01n1102170915
11215FS

9 780795 347566